KING LEAR

Text and Performance

GĀMINI SALGĀDO

MACMILLAN
EDUCATION

First published 1984
Reprinted 1987

Published by
MACMILLAN EDUCATION LTD
Houndmills, Basingstoke, Hampshire RG21 2XS
and London
Companies and representatives
throughout the world

Printed in Hong Kong

British Library Cataloguing in Publication Data
Salgādo, Gāmini
King Lear.–(Text and performance)
1. Shakespeare, William. King Lear
I. Title   II. Series
822.3′3   PR2819
ISBN 0–333–33996–7

CONTENTS

Illustrations will be found in Part Two

ACKNOWLEDGEMENTS

Quotations of the text of the play are from the New Penguin Shakespeare edition (1972), edited by G. K. Hunter.

[Gāmini Salgādo died shortly after the first publication of this book. His untimely death proves a great loss to contemporary Shakespearian studies. He is sadly missed.
—M.S.]

TO
FENELLA
WITH LOVE

GENERAL EDITOR'S PREFACE

For many years a mutual suspicion existed between the theatre director and the literary critic of drama. Although in the first half of the century there were important exceptions, such was the rule. A radical change of attitude, however, has taken place over the last thirty years. Critics and directors now increasingly recognise the significance of each other's work and acknowledge their growing awareness of interdependence. Both interpret the same text, but do so according to their different situations and functions. Without the director, the designer and the actor, a play's existence is only partial. They revitalise the text with action, enabling the drama to live fully at each performance. The academic critic investigates the script to elucidate its textual problems, understand its conventions and discover how it operates. He may also propose his view of the work, expounding what he considers to be its significance.

Dramatic texts belong therefore to theatre and to literature. The aim of the 'Text and Performance' series is to achieve a fuller recognition of how both enhance our enjoyment of the play. Each volume follows the same basic pattern. Part One provides a critical introduction to the play under discussion, using the techniques and criteria of the literary critic in examining the manner in which the work operates through language, imagery and action. Part Two takes the enquiry further into the play's theatricality by focusing on selected productions of recent times so as to illustrate points of contrast and comparison in the interpretation of different directors and actors, and to demonstrate how the drama has worked on the modern stage. In this way the series seeks to provide a lively and informative introduction to major plays in their text and performance.

MICHAEL SCOTT

PLOT SYNOPSIS AND SOURCES

I: Gloucester introduces his illegitimate son Edmund to a fellow-courtier, Kent. Lear decides to abdicate, sharing his kingdom among his three daughters in measure as they express their love for him. Goneril and Regan respond with hypocritical hyperbole, but the youngest, Cordelia, tersely affirms a duteous filial affection. Lear, wrathful, disowns her, banishes Kent for defending her and divides his realm between Goneril and Regan and their respective husbands, Albany and Cornwall. Cordelia marries the French king. Edmund plans to dispossess his legitimate brother Edgar by poisoning Gloucester's mind against him. Lear goes to live with Goneril. To be rid of him and his retinue she encourages her servant Oswald to be insolent. The disguised Kent enters Lear's service. After a furious quarrel with Goneril, Lear curses her and departs to Regan's castle.

II: Edmund convinces Gloucester of Edgar's disloyalty while persuading his brother to flee. Kent, on his way to Gloucester from Lear, quarrels with Oswald and is put in the stocks by Cornwall and Regan. Lear vainly protests at Kent's humiliation. Goneril arrives and the sisters insist that only Lear, without his knights, may lodge with them. Cursing, Lear departs into the stormy night.

III: In the storm Lear inveighs against mankind. With his Fool and Kent he enters a hovel where Edgar meets them, disguised as a mad beggar. The deranged Lear holds a 'trial' of his daughters. Cornwall, learning from Edmund of Gloucester's loyalty to Lear, blinds him and is mortally wounded by a nauseated servant. Gloucester discovers Edmund's treachery.

IV: With Edgar's help, Gloucester reaches Dover, where he intends to commit suicide. Edgar thwarts this and kills Oswald who plans Gloucester's death. They meet the mad king who is restored to sanity and reconciled with Cordelia, arrived with the French army.

V: The invading French forces are defeated, but Edgar wounds Edmund mortally in single combat. Dying, Edmund vainly tries to countermand his orders for the deaths of Lear and Cordelia. Goneril, jealous of Regan's love for Edmund, takes poison and dies. Edgar reveals himself and recounts his father's death. Lear enters bearing the dead Cordelia and dies, heartbroken, shortly after.

SOURCES

Elements in the story occur in Geoffrey of Monmouth, *Historia Regum Britanniae* (12th cent., with French and English translations) and in Raphael Holinshed, *Historie of England* (part of the *Chronicles* published by him, 1577) – both of which treat of a legendary King Lear. A more immediate source is the anonymous play *The True Chronicle of the History of King Leir and his daughters* (printed c. 1590, reprinted 1605). (Llyr, a Celtic sea-god, figures in the Welsh *Mabinogion*.)

PART ONE: TEXT

1 INTRODUCTION

The history of Shakespeare on the stage is very largely a record of abridgement and mutilation, sentimental prettification and its 'realistic' opposite. Though we know little or nothing of how Shakespeare was performed in his own time, the discrepancies between various versions of the same play, and all that we know of the relations between the playhouse and the printing house, indicate that there was nothing sacrosanct about the printed text of a play, Shakespearean or otherwise.*

This applies as much to the tragedies as to Shakespeare's other plays. Ever since Samuel Pepys commended the *Macbeth* he saw for the excellence of its music and dancing, such liberties have been taken with the great tragedies that, had they been less massively conceived and durably constructed, they could scarcely have survived them. But none of the major tragedies has suffered on the stage the kind of drastic transformation of the dramatist's original creation as has *King Lear*, arguably the greatest tragedy ever written.

For nearly a century and a half, until the great Victorian tragic actor William Macready restored to the stage in 1838 something akin to the original, what had been staged as the tragedy of *King Lear* was a version (published in 1681) by Nahum Tate, who had undertaken the task of 'improving' Shakespeare's play. Tate was not alone in the view that the play needed improving, for at that period drama, like other arts, was judged by certain rules of decorum, balance, good sense, and similar criteria. Shakespeare had clearly broken a good many of

---

* In Part Two, section 9 ('Selection and Emphasis'), I discuss textual aspects (including the relationship between the 1608 and 1623 printed versions of the play) as they relate to the 'material' with which producers and actors, as well as literary scholars and students, have to deal in understanding and interpreting *King Lear*. Some readers may wish to refer to this section at the outset, others to approach it in the context within which, in writing the book, I have found it convenient to place this kind of discussion.

these. That he may not have been aware of the existence of such rules might excuse the playwright but not the play.

His innate genius was acknowledged then as now, but he was seen as lacking 'art': and art was precisely what Tate set out to supply. In his own words: 'I found the whole . . . a Heap of Jewels, unstrung and unpolisht; yet so dazzling of their Disorder, that I soon perceiv'd I had seized a Treasure' (Dedication to his *King Lear*, 1681). Among the alterations which Tate saw fit to make in order 'to rectify what was wanting in the Regularity and Probability of the Tale' was the elimination of the Fool, the invention of a love intrigue between Edgar and Cordelia, and the survival of the latter and of Lear himself in a restored and reunited kingdom.

It is easy enough to see that Tate was engaged in a self-defeating task. He was trying to construct a tragedy for an age which had no tragic sense, only a superficial notion of tragic form. It is no accident that nothing of tragic drama that can be taken seriously has come down to us from that period, despite the fact that men of the calibre of Dryden, Congreve and Johnson attempted it. But what is more important than the fatuousness of Tate's enterprise is the fact that his version held the stage for so long and won the approval of critics as formidable as Samuel Johnson. This tells us a good deal about the distinctive qualities of *King Lear* among other Shakespearean tragedies and Jacobean tragedy generally.

Shakespeare's original audience had neither the inclination nor the vocabulary to theorise about what tragedy ought to be and do. They inherited what was essentially the medieval notion of tragedy as the fall of great men from prosperity to adversity. As Chaucer puts it in the Prologue to *The Monk's Tale*:

> Tragedie is to seyn a certeyn storie,
> As olde bokes maken us memorie,
> Of him that stood in greet prosperitie
> And is y-fallen out of heigh degree
> Into miserie, and endeth wrecchedly.

In its original pagan form the fall simply demonstrated the blind and unpredictable turnings of Fortune's wheel or, what amounted to the same thing, the arbitrary consequences on the human world of the strife between contending gods. But it was later seen as being regulated by divine providence which meted out just punishments for human wickedness, folly or pride. The tragic action typically culminated in the death of the protagonist, though this was not a necessary condition. Indeed, Shakespeare's chief dramatic source, the older play (c. 1590) of *King Leir* (though it was not labelled a tragedy in its printed form) shows both Lear and Cordelia surviving at the end. Because the tragic hero was usually a king or noble highly placed in society, his downfall had more general consequences on society as a whole. This is what Rosencrantz means when he addresses Claudius in lines reminiscent of one of the Fool's speeches in Lear:

> . . .   The cess of majesty
> Dies not alone, but like a gulf doth draw
> What's near it with it or 'tis a massy wheel
> Fixed on the summit of the highest mount,
> To whose huge spokes ten thousand lesser things
> Are mortised and adjoined; which when it falls,
> Each small annexment, petty consequence,
> Attends the boisterous ruin. . . .   [*Hamlet*, iii iii 15–22]

But out of the carnage and destruction which were part of the tragic rhythm there arose the vision of a new, restored order. Hamlet, Macbeth, Othello may die, but there is always a Fortinbras, a Malcolm or a Ludovico to pick up the pieces and start the process of rebuilding the new society

We can see without much reflection that Shakespeare's *King Lear* does not quite conform to these expectations, and that in some ways Tate's travesty does so rather better. For instance 'justice' is a word and an idea very central to Shakespeare's play, but few would say that a strong and unclouded sense of providential justice emerges from the play as a whole. This was what so disturbed Samuel Johnson; it made the ending of the tragedy almost too painful for re-reading and led him to prefer Tate's altered version. Again, while there is a growing sense of the wider social, political and even cosmic consequences of Lear's folly and fate, there is not anything like an equally marked feeling at the play's close of a new order coming into being. Compare the closing moments of *Macbeth* –

> . . .   What's more to do,
> Which would be planted newly with the time,
> As calling home our exiled friends abroad,
> That flew the snares of watchful tyranny,
> . . .
> . . .   – this, and what needful else
> That calls upon us, by the grace of Grace
> We will perform in measure, time, and place.
> So thanks to all at once, and to each one,
> Whom we invite to see us crowned at Scone.
>
> [v ix 30–3, 37–41]

– with its confident affirmation of final victory and vigorous
gaze towards future harmony, with the sense of exhausted
resignation which comes through in Edgar's final words in *King
Lear*:

> The weight of this sad time we must obey;
> Speak what we feel, not what we ought to say.
> The oldest hath borne most; we that are young
> Shall never see so much nor live so long.
>   *Exeunt with a dead march*   [v iii 321–4]

The speaker's own dim recognition that what he and we have
experienced is no ordinary stage tragedy seems to inform his
resolve to 'speak what we feel, not what we ought to say'.
Kenneth Muir has said that there is no such thing as
Shakespearean Tragedy, only Shakespearean tragedies; of no
play is this truer than *King Lear*.

Some Critical Approaches

Tate's transformation of Shakespeare's play is only the most
brutal instance of a persistent tendency to remould it in
accordance with the prejudices or preoccupations of the
remoulder. The theatrical results of this procedure are very
apparent and some of them will be discussed in Part Two. But
critical 'remakings', though perhaps less startling in their
immediate impact, can be every bit as radical. *King Lear* seems
to have a special power of invoking a wide-ranging, sometimes
baffling and often mutually contradictory, variety of critical
judgements. To catalogue them all would be impossible and

unhelpful, but some of the most important approaches demand brief discussion.

Both Tate's alteration of the play and Johnson's approval of that alteration were based on the perception that, in some deep and fundamental way, Shakespeare's tragedy offended against ideas of providential justice, especially in the ending. 'Shakespeare has suffered the virtue of Cordelia to perish', Johnson wrote, 'contrary to the ideas of natural justice.' It may therefore be surprising to discover that one influential line of criticism has insisted that Shakespeare's *King Lear* is nothing less than a Christian tragedy, if we understand the term rightly and keep in mind the essential meaning of the play rather than its accidental features. Such a view invariably and perhaps necessarily draws attention away from the actual structure of events which make up the tragedy – the disproportion, by any reasonable standards, between Lear's folly and his suffering, the even more monstrous disparity in the case of Gloucester, the gratuitousness of Cordelia's death, and so on – and concentrates on certain key passages which seem to have a redemptive or transcendental import.

Favourite examples are Cordelia's words, 'O dear father, / It is thy business that I go about' [IV iv 24–5], with their Biblical echo; the implications of resurrection to a new life in Lear's 'You do me wrong to take me out o' the grave' [IV vii 45]; and his great speech in the final act when all seems lost, beginning 'Come, let's away to prison' [v iii 8ff.]. Either Lear or Cordelia or both are seen as Christ-figures in this interpretation and the whole action as a broadly allegorical account of the human soul purged through suffering. Though A. C. Bradley was careful to insist that 'the constant presence of Christian beliefs would confuse or even destroy the tragic impression', this Christianising approach may fairly be traced to his great essay on the play, particularly to its final pages in which Bradley addresses the question: 'Why does Cordelia die?' His tentative answer is that her death (and Lear's) are a kind of triumph because

> the heroic being, though in one sense and outwardly he has failed, is in another sense superior to the world in which he appears; is in some way which we do not seek to define, untouched by the doom that overtakes him; and is rather set free from life than deprived of it.   (*Shakespearean Tragedy*, p. 270)

Bradley himself recognised that such a view, if pressed to its logical conclusion, would destroy the actuality of the tragic world and the reality and momentousness of the deaths of the tragic figures. But he maintained that in the case of Cordelia 'what happens to such a being does not matter; all that matters is what she is'. Some later critics, lacking Bradley's feeling for the reality of the play's action and therefore feeling no need for his reservations, have converted the play into a full-blown Christian drama, allegorical or otherwise. Inevitably such an approach tends to stress the final reconciliation and restoration of order far more than Bradley did, and more perhaps than we feel the play as a whole does. Bearing in mind the appalling cruelty of Cornwall and Regan, the suffering of Edgar as Poor Tom, and the senseless deaths of the Fool and Cordelia, not everyone will feel as convinced as John Danby that King Lear 'is at least as Christian as the *Divine Comedy*' (*Shakespeare's Doctrine of Nature*) – though Dante's masterpiece, of course, is not without its quota of horrors too.

Closely related to the Christian view of the play is what might be called the humanist approach. Briefly, this is the Christian interpretation shorn of any transcendental dimension, any reference to a celestial future in which the suffering of Lear and the sacrifice of Cordelia are redeemed and the cruelty of the wrong-doers punished. Instead, we are invited to see Lear's long agony as a necessary process in his moral education, and Cordelia as the embodiment of a purely human combination of integrity and charity. Though there is much suffering, it is not purely wanton, in that it gives us a more exalted sense of the human spirit and its potentialities. As Orwell (in his essay 'Lear, Tolstoy and the Fool') expresses it: 'Man is nobler than the forces which destroy him.' There is a meaning in suffering and therefore in human existence. The scope and implications of such a view are well represented in G. K. Hunter's Introduction to the New Arden edition of the play:

> At the beginning of the play he [Lear] is incapable of disinterested love, for he uses the love of others to minister to his own egotism. His prolonged agony and his utter loss of everything free his heart from the bondage of selfhood. He unlearns hatred, and learns love and humility. He loses the world and gains his own soul.

Regarding the vexed question of Cordelia's death, this kind of approach nearly always lays a heavy stress on Bradley's suggestion that Lear dies in an ecstasy of joy, believing Cordelia to be alive. We may feel that the humanist view is not so much wrong as inadequate to account for the peculiarly disturbing, rough-edged and deliberately unsymmetrical quality of the tragedy.

The 'psycho-analytic' approach, though not entirely unrepresented in modern criticism, has not found as much favour with respect to *King Lear* as it has with other Shakespearean tragedies, notably *Hamlet*. Freud himself remarked, sensibly enough, that the play was about the need to renounce authority and make friends with the necessity of dying. But it seems clear that *King Lear* does not invite the kind of detailed and sustained inquiry that would make a psychological approach profitable. Character seems to be cast in almost archetypal terms, and action tends to have a broadly representative quality. Indeed, the 'archetypal' or 'mythic' view of the play has been adopted by many critics.

Brief mention must also be made of the historical approach, which tries to recapture the play as it seemed to the original audience, with their religious, political and social ideas and prejudices. Strictly speaking, it is a logically impossible task, for we can never completely know a bygone age, and in any case we are oversimplifying when we talk of a single, homogeneous Elizabethan or Jacobean audience. But the attempt to regain a lost 'original' vision has often led to many acute insights which illuminate details of the play's action and language. Similarly, the outlook (deriving from and best exemplified in Harley Granville-Barker's famous 'Preface' to the play) which considers the play almost exclusively in terms of the playwright's craft, while obviously limited as a total response, has also yielded much valuable understanding.

Perhaps the most influential view of the play in recent times, at least as far as production has been concerned, is the so-called Absurdist interpretation expounded by Jan Kott in '*King Lear*, or Endgame', an essay in his widely discussed book *Shakespeare Our Contemporary* (1964). As his essay title suggests, Kott sees Shakespeare's tragedy as having the same general preoccupations as Beckett's drama, and even (or perhaps therefore) as

employing some of the same theatrical techniques. For
instance, he discusses in detail certain affinities between
passages in *Waiting for Godot* and the 'Dover cliff' scene in *Lear*
[IV vi]. Broadly speaking, the Absurdist view draws a distinction between the world of tragedy, where suffering is real but
also heroic, ennobling and therefore meaningful, and the world
of the 'grotesque', which poses the same questions as tragedy
(about the nature of suffering, man's relation to the gods and
the problem of pain and evil, among many others) but returns
radically different answers. *King Lear*, according to Kott, shows
us a tragic hero who is unaware that he inhabits the world of the
grotesque: a Job whose sufferings are unredeemed by the
existence of a finally omniscient and loving God. Kott sees
Gloucester's attempt to kill himself as the scene which defines
both the nature and scope of *King Lear*:

> Gloucester's suicide has meaning only if the gods exist. It is a
> protest against undeserved suffering and the world's injustice. . . .
> But if the gods, and their moral order in the world, do not exist,
> Gloucester's suicide does not solve or alter anything. It is only a
> somersault on an empty stage.

At a time when relativism and scepticism are widespread, and
no shared system of values is seen to operate, the Absurdist
view of *Lear* as a play which dramatises the absence of meaning
in life and the world, can be very persuasive. At any rate, as we
shall see in Part Two, it produced one of the most memorable
productions of Shakespeare's tragedy in our time.

2   FOOLS AND MADMEN, SAINTS AND MONSTERS

Lear as Fool and Madman

Different ways of looking at the play will naturally involve
different conceptions of the characters. The play itself indicates
in broad outline the position, age-group and attributes of a given
character, but the critic or director will flesh out these bald
details according to his own view of the play. In a very special

sense, the nature of character and identity looms large in *King Lear*, for not only the central character but the play itself repeatedly asks the question 'Who am I?' or more broadly 'What is man?' Is a king simply the man with the most power in society? ('A dog's obeyed in office' [IV vi 160–1].) Or is he a special kind of man whose authority derives from some innate distinction? ('You have that in your countenance', says the disguised Kent to Lear, 'which I would fain call master' [I iv].) Is man simply an upright animal in clothes, or is there such a thing as human nature? ('Is there any cause in nature that makes these hard hearts' [III vi 76–7].) Such questions reverberate throughout the play, haunting even those scenes where they are not directly raised.

In the simplest terms, Lear at the beginning of the play is a king, a father, a master and a man. As the action develops, the first three roles are stripped from him or distorted and he is forced to consider what the last of them means. He is also forced to adopt roles which he would rather shun. In the opening scene, where he is shown exercising his authority in three of his roles – king, father, master – he also commits an act of such rashness that we are forced to condone the Fool's judgement of him:

LEAR   Dost thou call me fool, boy?
FOOL   All thy other titles thou hast given away; that thou wast
            born with.   [I iv 147–8]

The fool, of course, speaks far more in earnest than in jest. Much of the ensuing action consists of Lear's desperate losing battle to prevent himself from recognising his deadly folly and its catastrophic consequences. Part of his resistance consists of an attempt to resume one of his original roles, that of supreme master. He does this by trying to exercise authority over his daughters and their household servants, and later by the awesome curses he calls down upon them. But the attempt is a failure, for the daughters remain callous and their lackeys unfeeling, and the invoked vengeance apparently does not come down on the fiendlike children.

It is Lear's folly and his refusal to accept it that leads directly to his madness, as he himself half glimpses. 'O Lear, Lear, Lear!' he cries, striking his head in despair. 'Beat at this gate

that let thy folly in / And thy dear judgement out!' [I iv 267–9] –
and later, with dreadful premonition, 'O let me not be mad, not
mad, sweet heaven!' [I v 43]. Lear's eventual lapse into lunacy is
triggered off by his encounter with a pretended madman, the
disguised Edgar. Why Edgar chooses this particular disguise is
perhaps not entirely clear in naturalistic terms, but it is his
effect on Lear that is notable. For it compels the king to
reconsider the most basic of his roles, that of mere man:

> Is man no more than this? Consider him well. Thou owest the
> worm no silk, the beast no hide, the sheep no wool, the cat no
> perfume. Ha! Here's three on's are sophisticated. Thou art the
> thing itself! Unaccommodated man is no more but such a poor,
> bare, forked animal as thou art. Off, off, you lendings! Come,
> unbutton here.
> *He tears off his clothes.*   [III iv 99–105]

Shakespeare's original audience may have found madness
amusing, but Shakespeare himself never portrays it for melodramatic effect or grotesque humour alone. In his madness Lear
enacts a bizarre travesty of his role as chief judge in his society,
but also utters some piercing truths about the nature of justice
and authority. It is one of the many paradoxes on which the
play is founded that Lear's judgement is folly and his madness
wisdom.

The Fool as Wise Man

The Fool not only repeatedly utters the paradox of wisdom and
folly, but embodies it in his own person. In creating him,
Shakespeare drew on two separate sources familiar in the social
life of the period. One was the natural fool, perhaps more
prevalent in pre-industrial communities where inbreeding was
fairly common. At one end of the scale such a person could be
slow-witted or simple-minded, at the other certifiably insane.
In most societies the natural fool has been treated with a
mixture of condescending pity and awe. An aura of mysterious
wisdom has clung to him, and he has been treated as one who is
somehow in touch with sources of wisdom and insight unavail-
able to the rational understanding. As the disguised Kent
remarks to Lear, 'This is not altogether fool, my lord' [I iv 149].

Occasionally the natural fool would find employment in a court or nobleman's household, where his sayings and antics entertained the assembled company. But there is no necessary connection between the licensed fool (or court jester) and the natural fool. In fact, the former had to be more than ordinarily quick-witted, as the anecdotes told of Will Summers, King Henry VIII's court jester, suggest, and as we can see in figures such as Feste in *Twelfth Night* and Touchstone in *As You Like It*. As his name indicates, the licensed fool was allowed a good deal of freedom of speech and action, and was not held responsible for them as other servants were. Indeed, his position within the household was somewhat ambiguous. Though a paid employee, he behaved more like the master's familiar friend, or perhaps a spoilt child, assuming in his behaviour and speech an equality of status which he did not in reality possess. No doubt the licensed fool sometimes took liberties which could not be tolerated by his betters and had to be punished, verbally or otherwise. 'Take heed sirrah, the whip', says Lear sharply to his Fool [I iv 109] when the latter speaks truths too painful to admit.

In uniting these two kinds of fool in a single figure, Shakespeare created a dramatic character of enormous depth and range. The Fool appears in only six of the twenty-six scenes of *King Lear* and he fades away well before the end of the third act; yet the entire play is full of his presence, right up to Lear's despairing line in his last speech, which, significantly, may refer equally to his beloved daughter: 'And my poor fool is hanged!' [v iii 303]. Part of the reason for the Fool's overwhelming impact is that he dramatises one of the play's chief concerns: namely, the nature of true folly and therefore of true wisdom. This brings him *dramatically* very close to the central figure, a closeness physically represented by much of the action and one which directors have often emphasised. As the action develops and we are made aware that the old king is a fool, we also come to realise that the Fool has a kind of wisdom, whose cutting edge is made keener by the gnomic and elliptical form which his utterances often take.

We are never quite sure exactly how much the Fool understands of what he says. The relevance of many of his words is immediately obvious. They spring not so much from any individual insight or experience but rather from a kind of immemorial communal wisdom, like proverbs. That is why his idiom often takes a proverbial turn – 'May not an ass know when the cart draws the horse?' [I iv 219–20] – or reminds us of folk poetry:

> Fathers that wear rags
> Do make their children blind,
> But fathers that bear bags
> Shall see their children kind.
> Fortune, that arrant whore,
> Ne'er turns the key to the poor.   [III iv 47–51]

Sometimes however, the Fool's words not only seem to have no particular application to the situation in hand but even to lack coherence, as if his wits too are giving way under the strain. At least once he seems to speak out directly to the audience:

> She that's a maid now, and laughs at my departure,
> Shall not be a maid long, unless things be cut shorter.
>   [I iv 48–9]

His occasional obscenity, as in the lines quoted above, contrasts sharply in its ribald jollity with the terrible sexual disgust of Lear's rantings. But the Fool too has his own vision of a general corruption and decay:

> When priests are more in word than matter,
> When brewers mar their malt with water,
> When nobles are their tailors' tutors,
> No heretics burned but wenches' suitors –
>   Then shall the realm of Albion
>   Come to great confusion.
>   . . .   [III ii 81–6]

As important as what the Fool says is what he does. He is savagely and unremittingly satirical about Lear's folly, and no less about the folly of clinging to great men after they have fallen from power – yet he does precisely this, remaining faithfully by his master's side in every extremity until death itself. In doing so he truly sets a pattern of folly, if wisdom consists of putting self-interest first and foremost. But it is a folly which is touched with a kind of saintliness, as if he were indeed a holy fool. It reminds us of another sublimely foolish figure, Cordelia.

Willfullness

Forms of Folly and Madness: Cordelia, Gloucester, Edgar

Like the Fool, Cordelia has an impact on the play and the audience out of all proportion to the scanty number of words she utters. In the opening scene of the play, her silence speaks louder than the treacly eloquence of her sisters. The whole scene moves from a series of rhetorical flourishes, beginning with Lear's grandly formal speech – 'Meantime we shall express our darker purpose' [I i 36] – and taking in his lyrical descriptions of the land as well as the hypocritical effusions of his elder daughters; then to Cordelia's deafening refusal to speak, and out again into the frenzied explosion of Lear's curse against her and his banishment of Kent. And yet Cordelia is not quite silent. Rather, her first words announce her determination not to speak – 'What shall Cordelia speak? Love, and be silent' [I i 62] – and her next brief speech gives us the reason:

> . . .   Since I am sure my love's
> More ponderous than my tongue.   [I i 77–8]

No doubt there is a streak of wilfulness in Cordelia – after all, she is her father's daughter. But we should not place too much emphasis on this aspect of her character. The scene surely involves us not so much in why Cordelia behaves the way she does, as in what her behaviour signifies and what it leads to. We shall consider shortly the implications of Cordelia's refusal to please her father by flattering him. Here we need to note that the single word 'Nothing' with which she responds to Lear's invitation is one that echoes and re-echoes throughout the play. Immediately after it is first spoken by Cordelia, it is repeated four times in three lines. It is one of those words – 'nature', 'man', 'justice' and 'blindness' are others – which seem to gather into themselves much of the meaning and power of the tragedy.

The affinity between the Fool and Cordelia comes out at many points and directors often emphasise it (as in Adrian Noble's production of 1982 at Stratford, when an opening tableau showed the two of them playing a childish game together). We are told that the Fool has pined a great deal since Cordelia went to France. We never see the two on stage together (it is possible that the same actor originally played both parts), and, as noted earlier, Lear's final lament could apply equally to both. All this suggests a rough parallelism between the two characters and their relationship to the tragic protagonist.

It seems clear that both Cordelia and the Fool are favourite children of Lear, one literally, the other in a figurative sense. From both he expects the indulgence he has shown towards them and a flattering self-image. At a crucial moment both cruelly disappoint him, Cordelia by refusing to flatter, the Fool by persistently making his master face up to unpalatable realities. Thus we may speak of both Cordelia and the Fool as aspects of Lear's conscience and consciousness. Their 'folly' acts as a background against which his own vaster unwisdom stands out in tragic relief.

Cordelia's initial 'folly' in refusing to utter honeyed words like her sisters is the beginning of Lear's long and painful journey through madness into self-knowledge. For Cordelia herself, it is the first stage in a martyr's progress that begins in prosperity – marriage to one who truly loves and values her, a share in the throne of a fair kingdom, and the opportunity to restore her father to health and sanity – but ends in suffering and death. To the end she maintains the independence of spirit which is so striking a feature not only of her response to Lear but also of her parting words to her sisters:

> . . .   I know you what you are;
> And, like a sister, am most loath to call
> Your faults as they are named. . . .   [I i 269–71]

Perhaps there is even a trace of self-righteousness here, though it is the clarity of perception that is most apparent. Like the Fool, Cordelia too is faithful in folly till death itself.

Gloucester's folly is of a more worldly kind, though its consequences are just as fatal. It would be unjust to the unsentimental but compassionate vision of the play to regard either Lear or Gloucester as deserving his fate. One of the realities the play asks us to face is that of a world where there is no conceivable proportion between the punishment and the offence. Doubtless there is something slightly off-colour in the old man's boasting about his youthful lechery, and certainly it is unwise of him to refer to Edmund in the terms he does in the latter's presence. But to consider Gloucester (or Lear) as meriting his terrible suffering is to blind ourselves to a good deal of the play's meaning. Gloucester can be fairly convicted of folly for his inability to see through Edmund's deceitfulness and his readiness to believe ill of Edgar. He is also too willing to impute blame for human actions on planetary dispositions, though many of Shakespeare's original audience would probably have thought this quite reasonable.

But Gloucester's real 'folly' and that which brings him close to the saintly folly of Cordelia and the Fool, is his final stand against deliberate human evil. Admittedly he is now powerless, but faced with the prospect of imminent torture, he refuses to co-operate with his captors and speaks out fearlessly. 'Wherefore to Dover?', Regan and her fiendish husband repeatedly ask him, to which he replies, with unconscious prescience of his own appalling fate:

> Because I would not see thy cruel nails
> Pluck out his poor old eyes; nor thy fierce sister
> In his anointed flesh rash boarish fangs.   [III vii 55–7]

Like Lear, Gloucester survives not only to bemoan his follies but to accept them and win through to a bleak and painful clarity.

Edgar is the last of the 'holy fools' in the play and in many ways the most awkward. To begin with, his gullibility towards his illegitimate brother is scarcely credible and almost makes us put him down for a fool pure and simple, except that the play soon shows us that there is no such thing. Secondly, the reasoning behind his choice of disguise is obscure. But once he is transformed into a Bedlam beggar, his words within that role have an undeniable evocative power. He paints a vivid picture of the society of his day, from the 'serving man, proud in heart and mind, that curled my hair, wore gloves in my cap, served the lust of my mistress' heart and did the act of darkness with her' [III iv 82–4] to 'Poor Tom . . . who is whipped from tithing to tithing and stock-punished and imprisoned' [III iv 127–9]. His assumed insanity contrasts sharply with Lear's genuine madness – though, as with Hamlet, there are moments, especially where Edgar is tending his blinded father, when we wonder how much he is really in control of his assumed role.

The immediate effect of Edgar's appearance during the storm
scene is, of course, to impel Lear towards a consideration of the
'essential' nature of man, if he has any. Edgar's idiom reaches
down into the dark depths of superstition and folk lore:

> This is the foul fiend Flibbertigibbet. He begins at curfew and
> walks till the first cock. He gives the web and the pin, squinies the
> eye and makes the harelip, mildews the white wheat, and hurts the
> poor creature of earth.   [III iv 110–14]

In this he is akin to the Fool. His plight leads Lear, in the very
depths of his madness, to a consideration of the nature of
earthly justice and to insights which, though crazed, are shot
through with a piercing lucidity. Thus we return to the paradox
of folly and madness leading to a kind of wisdom.

Perhaps the play asks Edgar to enact too great a diversity of
roles, which may be why he is so often colourless and only
intermittently convincing on stage. Beginning as the dutiful but
dull son, he is speedily transformed from credulous victim to
pretended madman and 'unconscious' satirist, then into a
yokel, and lastly to a knightly champion who saves the realm
from tyranny. His tendency to moralise over other people's
sufferings is very marked and strikes us as something that
comes rather too easily to him, as when he tells Edmund:

> . . .
> The gods are just, and of our pleasant vices
> Make instruments to plague us:
> The dark and vicious place where thee he got
> Cost him his eyes.   [v iii 168–71]

The faint priggishness of many of his sententious remarks
reminds us of the disturbing self-righteousness of some of
Cordelia's. It is therefore fitting that it is Edgar himself who
speaks the play's final lines, with their clear-eyed recognition
that the tragedy is too overwhelming to be neatly parcelled up
with moralising tags.

The Characters of Evil: The Wicked Sisters, Cornwall, Edmund

It is quite appropriate that we should think of Goneril and
Regan partly in fairy-tale terms as 'the wicked sisters', for there

is a distinct air of folk tale about *King Lear*. It has the broad simplicity of conception, the massive authority and something of the formal patterning, of anonymous communal narrative. But we should not make the mistake of imagining that there is anything naïve or over-simple about the play's presentation of evil.

The full extent of the older sisters' wickedness is only gradually revealed. In fact, the apparent reasonableness of their behaviour has often been emphasised in production. Shakespeare takes care to give them a case, though some modern directors may have overstated it. In the opening scene, their protestations certainly strike us as excessive, but need not for that reason be condemned outright. After all, Lear wants fine words, and where is the harm in humouring an old man who happens to be both your father and an absolute monarch? Their silence in the face of Cordelia's question – 'Why have my sisters husbands if they say / They love you all?' [I i 99–100] – and of her references to their 'glib and oily art' may show dignity and self-restraint. It is only when they are left alone at the end of the scene that their real natures, as opposed to their public masks, are revealed.

Shakespeare makes sure we will mark the change by dropping sharply from high-flown rhetorical verse to prose of the most chillingly pragmatic kind. In this exchange we see Goneril as the more forceful of the pair, the one who takes the initiative and wants to strike while the iron is hot ('We must do something, and i' th' heat' [I i 306]), while her sister is more cautious. But both are quite clear-eyed in their appraisal of their father's folly and their own good fortune, all the more welcome for being unexpected, since their father had 'always loved our sister most'. They realise the need to turn Lear's rashness to their own advantage.

> . . . Pray you, let us hit together. If our father carry authority with such disposition as he bears, this last surrender of his will but offend us.   [I i 301–4]

The deadly reasonableness of first one then the other sister's complaint against their father may not be ignored. Lear striking one of Goneril's gentlemen for rebuking his Fool, his attack on Oswald, his intemperate railing, all these would undoubtedly be provoking to a hostess, though we must not forget that Goneril has deliberately set Oswald on to be insolent to the king. There is no evidence in the play of any riotous behaviour on the part of Lear's retinue. Lear himself vehemently denies the charge [I iv 260–3], and certainly one of the knights sounds puzzled at the change of attitude towards his master which he has detected: 'My Lord, I know not what the matter is but to my judgement your highness is not entertained with that ceremonious affection as you were wont' [I iv 56–8]. But the request for a reduction of the train, in spite of a public undertaking to maintain Lear's hundred knights, may not be altogether unreasonable in the circumstances. Why then does his daughters' offer to look after Lear with their own servants alone make our blood run cold?

It is the single-mindedness with which Goneril and Regan pursue the goal of self-interest, with no regard to the suffering and cruelty they inflict on others, which finally appals us. When those others include father, husband (in Goneril's case) and host, we can no longer be in doubt as to what they really are. It is a quality which Regan shares not only with her sister but with her husband Cornwall, whom Gloucester describes to the king as 'fiery . . . immovable and fixed . . . to his own course' [II iv 88–90]. Cornwall has a worldly shrewdness which makes him suspect the disguised Kent of being one of those who trade on their reputation for plain speaking, and a keen eye for the main chance, as well as a relish for cruelty surpassed only by his wife. He provides a sharp contrast to Albany, whom the mounting outrages convert from a timid onlooker to a fearless defender of threatened values. In the hideous scene of Gloucester's blinding it is not Cornwall but Regan, hitherto the weaker sister, who provides the crowning moment of horror. 'One eye will mock another', she shrieks, 'th' other too!' [III vii 70]. In the 1982 Stratford production (directed by Adrian Noble) there was a terrifying touch when, Regan, just before speaking those lines, coolly took out the pin from her elaborately coiffeured hair and handed it to her husband with all the care of a nurse handing an instrument to an operating surgeon.

The sisters and Cornwall pursue evil and embody it, but make no attempt to explain it or justify it – as Iago, for instance, does in *Othello*. Here that task falls to Edmund and, in so far as it is possible, he performs it brilliantly. The change from the modest and courteous young man of the first scene to the eloquent spokesman for 'Nature' and bastards in the second [1 ii 1–22] is almost as great as the change from verse to prose of the two sisters. Edmund vindicates himself against his legitimate brother by elaborating one of the fashionable paradoxes of the time (see New Penguin edition, p. 19). But his defence is not merely that of the bastard's right to greater regard from society because of his superior vitality. If it were, he would be an isolated figure in the world of the play, like Iago. Edmund becomes the spokesman for all the villainous characters in the play by laying bare the assumptions on which he and they alike base their actions. He invokes Nature as his 'goddess', but it is a Nature far removed from that which Lear appeals to in his dreadful curse against Goneril ('Hear, Nature, hear' [1 iv 272]). Edmund's Nature is one which refuses to recognise ties of blood, traditional sanctities ('the curiosity of nations') or any system of values except that of amoral, purposeful energy. It is very like what is invoked by Lear in disowning Cordelia [1 i 113–20] where he 'disclaim[s] all [his] paternal care, / Propinquity and property of blood'. Anything, in Edmund's view, is justified as long as it succeeds in getting you where you want to be ('All with me's meet that I can fashion fit' [1 ii 180]). The man who knows the way of the world knows that only fools take moral principles and obligations seriously, and fools exist only so that cannier men can exploit their gullibility on their way to the top. If fortune and men's eyes are lost in the process, so much the worse for them.

There is something strikingly 'modern' as well as undeniably attractive in Edmund's no-nonsense air of clearing away the accumulated rubbish of uncritically accepted assumptions, as well as in his acknowledgement of self-responsibility: 'I should have been that I am had the maidenliest star in the firmament twinkled on my bastardising' [1 ii 130–2]. But we should be careful to note the consequences of this attitude as the play shows them. Edmund and his cronies succeed well enough to begin with, and the world does seem to go according to their beliefs. What finally undoes him and them is not only the existence of those to whom self-interest is not the most important value in life – Kent, Cordelia, the anonymous

servant who loses his life in a vain bid to save Gloucester from
further torture – but the self-destructiveness inherent in evil.
When all constraints of family, society, law, religion and
morality are abandoned, we are left with naked appetites, lust
and the lust for power. When these come into collision with the
competing lusts and ambitions of other amoral 'realists', the
result is, predictably, internecine strife and mutual annihila-
tion. The sisters destroy themselves because of their deadly
passion for Edmund, while Edmund himself, defeated and
dying, recognises the logic that has brought him down: 'Th'
hast spoke right', he tells Edgar, ''Tis true. The wheel is come
full circle; I am here' [v iii 171–2].

King Lear clearly shows us that innocence, courage, loyalty
and love are in themselves no sufficient armour against
overweening egotism, cruelty and the ruthless pursuit of power;
but equally clearly the play shows that these latter attributes
are no armour against themselves and the destruction they
wreak.

universal

3   THE WORLDS OF THE PLAY

Lear's Quarrel with Cordelia

King Lear opens, not with the great scene of the division of the
kingdom, but with the quieter exchange between Gloucester
and Kent, with the former's bastard son Edmund hovering
obsequiously in the background. This short prelude does
several things at once. It introduces both the main plot and the
sub-plot economically, and it gives us a fair idea of the
characters of Gloucester and Edmund. But it also tells us that
the impending division of the kingdom is common knowledge,
at least at Court, and, in the contrast in dramatic language,
emphasises the fact that the division scene is a *public* occasion.
Our understanding of what happens should be partly guided
by this perception.

The scene has a formality of speech and gesture which befits
the situation. We need not concern ourselves too much with

questions of probability when considering the action. As so often, Shakespeare is only concerned with happenings for the insight that can be gained through them and not for their statistical likelihood. In any case, a dramatist has the freedom to begin with whatever situation his imagination seizes upon as long as he develops it with consistency and sympathetic understanding. After all, Pirandello asks us to believe in the 'reality' of six characters who have escaped to the theatre from an abandoned novel (*Six Characters in Search of an Author*), and Ionesco in that of a corpse whose leg keeps growing till it occupies a whole apartment (*Amédée, or How to Get Rid of It*). Lear's insistent need for flattery and Cordelia's refusal of it will trouble us only if we are straitjacketed by the narrowest notions of 'lifelikeness'.

The terms in which Lear puts his question are unmistakably material and quantitative:

> . . .   Tell me, my daughters,
> Which of you shall we say doth love us most,
> That we our largest bounty may extend
> Where nature doth with merit challenge.
> . . .   [I i 48–53]

Goneril's response shows that she has grasped the full implications of the question, for it is expressed entirely in terms of a comparative estimate, with the key terms of the comparison ('word' and 'matter') given in the very first line. It is also notable for the fourfold repetition of the word 'love' and the equation of 'love' with 'value'. Goneril's comparisons still have a semi-abstract air about them ('grace, health, beauty, honour') which her competing sister hardens into currency:

> I am made of that self mettle as my sister
> And price me at her worth. In my true heart
> I find she names my very deed of love;
> Only she comes too short . . .   [I i 69–72]

Each of them easily wins the prize she plays for. In barely fifty lines the word 'love' has been heard a dozen times. Its repetitions in the mounting waves of flattery and self-love collide with a deafening impact against the rock-hard resistance of Cordelia's 'Nothing'. From now till the very last moment of the tragedy these two words 'love' and 'noth-

ing' will reverberate in our minds and hearts as we hear
them uttered by different characters in bizarre, surprising
and heart-rending contexts. Not all these can be discussed
or even noted here, but some of the crucial instances need
comment.

Running through the use of the word 'love' in this scene and
in the play as a whole is a pun which is lost to us but was
probably available to the original audience. As Terence
Hawkes has shown, the word combined two senses which come
from two separate Old English words, one meaning 'to
appraise, estimate or state the price or value of' and the other
having the modern sense of 'feeling affection for'. (His essay is
reproduced in the Casebook on the play, pp. 178–83: see
Reading List, below.) Perhaps the first sense is uppermost
when Cordelia says: 'I love your majesty / According to my
bond, no more nor less' [I i 92–3]. It certainly lurks behind her
sisters' easy equation of love and quantitative value and is there
in Lear's very question.

Cordelia's refusal to flatter may be seen as an insistence on the
difference, indeed the incompatibility between the two senses
of 'love'. There may even be a connection between an older,
more traditional, way of life in which 'pricing' was not common
because things were made to be used, not to be sold for money,
and a newer more commercial society (such as that of
Shakespeare's own age) in which everything, including men
themselves, had a definite and statable 'exchange value', and a
man of 'worth' or 'substance' was such in a specific material
sense. At any rate it is the more traditional figures, such as
Cordelia, Gloucester and Kent, who adhere to the idea of love
as non-material affection while the newer, more thrusting
figures in society – the sisters, Edmund and Cornwall – see men
and affairs solely in terms of quantity.

Certainly there is a touch of coldness about Cordelia's
assertion that in loving her father she is only doing her duty, but
it is a coldness to which she is driven by the fulsome and
calculating flattery to which she has been listening. There is
even a touch of mockery, I think, in her *reductio ad absurdum* of
the idea of love as a measurable and therefore divisible entity,
like a cake:

> Why have my sisters husbands, if they say
> They love you all? Haply when I shall.wed,
> That lord whose hand must take my plight shall carry
> Half my love with him, half my care and duty.   [ɪ i 99–102]

Lear's admonition, which provokes his youngest daughter to this speech, reiterates the assumption on which his question is based, by asking her to 'mend your speech a little, lest you may mar your fortunes' [ɪ i 94–5]. Cordelia's stance is therefore not to be accounted for in terms of the stubbornness of a spoilt child but as a *public* affirmation of moral distinctions and values which she believes are being publicly threatened and degraded. She speaks, not as a private individual, but on behalf of a whole world of value and order.

Like the word 'love', the word 'nothing' undergoes many repetitions, the more marked in this scene because they come so close together. 'Nothing will come of nothing', warns Lear [ɪ i 90], and the entire action can be seen as an exploration of that remark. In the sub-plot Gloucester, in an apparently trivial context, makes the analogous comment that 'the quality of nothing has not such need to hide itself' [ɪ ii 34]. Both Lear and Gloucester must become 'nothing' before the upward, redemptive movement of the tragedy can begin; and Edgar, the principal agent of the redemption, at the lowest point of his fortune as 'poor Tom' begins with the realisation that 'Edgar I nothing am' [ɪɪ iii 21]. Lear's 'nothing' comes not out of nothing but, literally, out of the 'everything' he gave his two daughters, for it is because of their swift reduction of his train from a hundred knights to none at all that he is forced to ask himself the agonising questions about human need and human identity which in turn lead him to the 'nothingness' of 'Off, off, you lendings! Come, unbutton here' [ɪɪɪ iv 105].

The nothing that Cordelia offered is seen to be rich in what is most humanly valuable – pity, affection, tenderness, care – and in the end, when Lear has been robbed of these by her death, he truly has nothing. In a tragedy heavy with ironies, perhaps the most poignant irony is that Lear, who turned a deaf ear to his true-speaking youngest daughter when she was alive, now vainly strains his ear to catch the sound of her voice 'soft, gentle and low'.

Language and Silence

The paradox embodied by Cordelia and her sisters in the opening scene – namely, that the most eloquent language hides emptiness and evil while love and value reside in near-silence – is echoed and re-echoed in many different contexts throughout the tragedy. Ironically enough, the notion that language is inadequate to express the weight of true feeling is first uttered by Goneril ('Sir, I love you more than words can wield the matter') and repeated with emphasis by her sister: 'I find she names my very deed of love; / Only she comes too short' [i i 71–2]. It is of course a very old rhetorical trick to claim that words cannot do justice to one's true feelings on the importance of the matter at issue. But Shakespeare uses this very device almost as a structural principle of the play and achieves a kind of eloquence that seems to lie beyond eloquence, a paradox within a paradox, so to speak. At most of the great moments in the drama, the idea of the inadequacy of words is either directly expressed or embodied in the action.

At the beginning authority and eloquence seem to be embodied in the person of Lear, as we can see in the confident rhythm of his speeches and later in the strength of his commands and curses, still backed by regal power. Cordelia's perception that truth can express itself in this debased world only in silence and paradox is applied to herself in the king of France's words:

> Fairest Cordelia, that art most rich, being poor,
> Most choice, forsaken, and most loved, despised.
>
> [i i 250–1]

This is followed by the menacingly matter-of-fact exchanges between the sisters, in which the language is ruthlessly impersonal, like a clinical report on Lear, while Edmund's 'manifesto' speech, for all its engaging forthrightness, once more associates the power of words with a single-minded egotism.

The only kind of 'eloquence' which dares to express itself in the atmosphere of growing treachery and cruelty is the gnomic eloquence of folly and madness. In the scraps of rhyme and garbled proverbs of the Fool, and in the more sustained ravings

of Poor Tom which themselves prefigure Lear's later mad
utterances, we can apprehend truths which are profoundly
relevant to the play's meanings, but we can only do so
tentatively, as through a glass darkly. The Fool's words have a
symbolic aptness:

> Truth's a dog must to kennel; he must be whipped out when the
> Lady Brach may stand by the fire and stink.   [I iv 110–15]

It is with Goneril's first open challenge to Lear's authority that
the division between power and eloquence begins to manifest
itself clearly. Lear's initial response to this challenge is
characteristic of many he makes throughout the play, in that it
seems to go beyond the immediate occasion and raise issues of
universal importance, in this case about the nature of identity
and genuine understanding:

> Does any here know me? This is not Lear.
> Does Lear walk thus, speak thus? Where are his eyes?
> Either his notion weakens, his discernings
> Are lethargied – Ha! Waking? 'Tis not so!
> Who is it that can tell me who I am?   [I iv 222–6]

In the disjointed syntax, and in the monosyllabic simplicity of
the last line we can sense, in retrospect, the first signs of that
progressive rejection of words as adequate 'bearers' of tragic
experience which is the hallmark of the play.

Further evidence of the growing gap between language and
real power comes when Lear swears to have 'such revenges'
against his daughters as 'shall be the terrors of the earth' and
yet cannot say what they are [II iv 274–6]. More and more the
play seems to suggest that actions alone are the true test of
human life and that language inevitably breaks down under the
pressure of overwhelming experience. Thus, after Lear's wild
ravings during the storm, he encounters poor Tom and with
him a question of elemental directness: 'Is man no more than
this?' But the answer to that fundamental dilemma finds its real
expression not so much in words as in the action which
accompanies them: 'Off, off, you lendings! Come, unbutton
here.' Words and action are here equally bare, as they are when
Lear, restored to sanity, wakes up to find his youngest
daughter. 'Sir, do you know me?', Cordelia tenderly inquires,

to which her father's equally direct if mistaken answer is: 'You
are a spirit, I know. Where did you die?' When he slowly learns
the truth, words almost fail him: 'I know not what to say.'

The gods themselves are silent or speak with the irreducible
ambiguity of thunder. The structure of human language,
already fractured in folly and madness, now collapses (after the
brief, beautiful and lucid interval of 'Come, let's away to
prison') till in the final scene the only recourse seems to be
repetition, as if uttering a word or phrase over and over again
could somehow enable the sufferer to extract some bearable
meaning from it. 'Howl, howl, howl!', cries the anguished Lear,
and later, 'No, no, no life', and – faced with the appalling
simplicity of

> Why should a dog, a horse, a rat have life,
> And thou no breath at all? . . .   [v iii 304–5]

– the futile, five times repeated 'Never' seems more like the
banging of a head against a wall than human utterance, leading
to the final pathetic, deluded action which once again sup-
plants words: the call for a mirror to test whether Cordelia is
still breathing. Small wonder that Edgar in the closing lines
feels the need somehow to find words to 'speak what we feel', for
the entire play shows a relentless and steadily accumulating
scepticism about the claims of language to express adequately
the extremity of human experience.

Power and Nakedness, Blindness and Insight

One of the many permanently relevant questions which *King
Lear* explores is the nature of power, its perils and possibilities.
There is a profound contradiction, or perhaps two contradic-
tions, at the heart of Lear's initial resolve to give up the crown
and divide his kingdom among his daughters and their
husbands. In the first place, he does not really want to renounce
power but merely to relieve himself of the duties and respon-
sibilities that should accompany it. He wishes to 'shake all
cares and business from our age' and yet 'retain the name and
all th' addition of a king'. He learns the bitter truth that in the
real world these are incompatible aims. Secondly, his motives

in dividing the kingdom are impure. He does not wish to do so
because he believes this is a wise or just thing to do, but in order
to 'test' his daughters' love for him. How tragically ineffectual
is the test constitutes Lear's other grim lesson.

The process by which Lear discovers the tragic implications
of his original decision is presented in the play in a number of
ways. Among the most important of these is the visual
metaphor of clothes being gradually stripped off until only the
naked human body is left in answer to the question: 'Is man no
more than this?' As suggested above, this theme finds a parallel
in the progressive denudation of language from rhetorical
richness to the stark, rocky directness of 'unaccommodated'
speech. But it is more immediately present in the imagery of
clothes and naked flesh which is evident throughout the play
and in the unfolding action itself.

In the opening scene we see Lear decked out in all the pomp
of absolute royal authority, and this is followed by the scenes in
his daughters' households where he would still be attired, if not
in ceremonial robes, at least in garments befitting his kingly
rank. Significantly, Lear's climactic protest against the humiliation he is undergoing finds expression in an outburst at the
extravagance and uselessness of Regan's apparel when judged
against the criterion of human 'need':

> O, reason not the need! Our basest beggars
> Are in the poorest thing superfluous.
> Allow not nature more than nature needs –
> Man's life is cheap as beast's. Thou art a lady;
> If only to go warm were gorgeous,
> Why, nature needs not what thou gorgeous wear'st,
> Which scarcely keeps thee warm. . . .   [II iv 259–65]

In the storm scenes Lear becomes more and more dishevelled
till, encountering the opposite extreme in terms of clothing to
the ladylike finery of Regan in the wild raggedness of Poor
Tom, he realises that he was wrong to think that 'our basest
beggars are in the poorest thing superfluous'. Man's life, Lear
now feels, is as cheap as a beast's, and is driven to reduce
himself to the condition of bestial nakedness. This is the lowest
point of his physical degradation from which he slowly rises,
first as a kind of nature figure crowned with flowers and the

weeds 'that grow in our sustaining corn', and more positively when he is given new clothes and wakes to music in Cordelia's care.

The verbal and visual imagery of clothing is closely related to two other important strands in the play. One, already mentioned in passing, is that of the naked flesh, which in turn links up with all the powerful images of different parts of the human body – the frequent references to eye, heart and brain, scenes such as the blinding of Gloucester (which we shall return to shortly), Lear's crazed injunction to 'let them anatomise Regan, see what breeds about her heart', and many others. This helps to make the impact of the events both universal in its implications and intimately personal in its effect. Secondly, the clothing imagery, through the idea of stripping down to essentials, links up with one of the most pregnant themes in the play: that of Nothing. Nothing, as Northrop Frye pointed out, functions in the play in two distinct but related senses, first as the absence of anything and then as a thing called Nothing. (His study is reproduced in the Casebook on the play, p. 268.) In a sense, as I have already implied, the whole action can be seen as a refutation of Lear's glib judgement that 'Nothing will come of nothing'. It is out of the 'nothing' that Lear bestows on Cordelia that all his misfortunes stem; but it is also out of the 'Nothing' which Cordelia utters that salvation finally comes. Moreover, it is not until Lear has become 'nothing' that he can begin the long and painful struggle towards true humanity. Reduction has to precede renewal.

At least one other unifying image-idea, or cluster of image-ideas, needs to be noted: namely, those of sight, blindness, imperception and insight. Like the other strands of thought and imagery, these find verbal as well as visual expression, the most obvious visual representation being the scene of the blinding of Gloucester. The horrifying details of the presentation make it impossible for us to evade its reality by any glib talk of its 'symbolic' value. It is about deliberate, naked, sadistic, human cruelty, and any account of it which failed to recognise this would be false to its true quality. It is also true, however, that the scene gathers into itself some of the play's deepest insights and ironies, and that its significance spills over from the sub-plot to the main action. From the moment when Kent implores Lear to 'see better', 'and let me still remain the true blank of thine eye', the paradox of those who, seeing, see not, is persistent in both stories. In the sub-plot it reaches its climax in Gloucester's 'I have no way and therefore want no eyes; I stumbled when I saw' [IV i 18–19] – which of course directly applies to Lear, too. In the encounter between the blind Gloucester and the crazy king and in Lear's taunting of the blind man ('I remember thine eyes well enough'), the verbal and visual resonances of both stories come together with a terrible poignancy and generate a further connection between the ideas of apparent madness and genuine insight.

Thus, though one may artificially and temporarily separate one thread of imagery or ideas for discussion, the play itself, in the closeness and complexity of its interweaving, finally frustrates any effort to unravel its unity.

Beyond Tragedy: The Death of Cordelia

Nahum Tate's version of *King Lear*, in which Cordelia does not die but is happily married to Edgar at the end, held the stage for over a century and a half. This fact is worth reflecting on with something more than amused retrospective superiority. During those one hundred and fifty-odd years, theatre audiences varied a great deal in social and educational level and in intellectual, theatrical and moral sophistication; yet they all apparently found Tate's ending not only acceptable but superior to Shakespeare's. Why? There are two relevant points to bear in mind. Samuel Johnson himself found the ending of the play too painful for re-reading, and most of Shakespeare's sources did not contain the death of Cordelia.

All of this suggests, first, that for whatever reason Shakespeare deliberately altered his sources in respect of the ending; and secondly, that most audiences (till fairly recent times anyway) have felt that the ending he chose was in some way unusual and even repellent. In attempting to explore the reasons for this we can understand something both of the unique structure of *King Lear* and of its relation to what we usually think of as dramatic tragedy.

In most tragedies, the central character suffers, usually

through some error of judgement or 'fatal flaw' in his make-up, and, typically, dies. But at the end we are made to feel that his sufferings have somehow purified or ennobled him, that his death is in some way an affirmation of life's highest values, and is accompanied by a greater understanding and insight on his own part. In other Shakespearean tragedies there is also, at the end, some kind of recognition, either by the hero himself or by some other character, of the hero's achievement or potential. Thus we have Fortinbras's tribute to Hamlet or Octavius's to Antony or Othello's exalted retrospect of himself. Finally, there is a clear indication of a restoration of order after the chaotic events of the tragedy, best seen perhaps at the end of *Macbeth*.

If we consider *King Lear* with these expectations in mind, we find the play does not quite fulfil them. Or rather, it over-fulfils them, so to speak, leading us beyond the point of tragic illumination and the restoration of order to a darker and more problematic area. It is easy enough to see the 'normal' tragic pattern in the play. Lear, at the beginning, is guilty of a hideous error of judgement and suffers accordingly. Through his suffering he learns to shed his pride and egoism and accept his common humanity and the value of the love he at first rejected. But it is at this point that the tragic pattern begins to diverge from our expectations. For the climax of Lear's 'education' and acceptance of true values comes in the great speech just before Lear and Cordelia are led away as captives. Lear has lost everything – crown, kingdom, possessions – but he has gained the one thing he now most wants, the love and company of his beloved daughter. The confident serenity of his speech denotes the completeness of his joy in the bargain as he invites his daughter to join him

> And take upon's the mystery of things
> As if we were God's spies; and we'll wear out,
> In a walled prison, packs and sects of great ones
> That ebb and flow by the moon.   [v iii 16–19]

But this speech comes at the *beginning* of Act v and two of the decisive events of the tragedy are yet to come: the death of Cordelia and the subsequent death of Lear. Putting it simply, yet not too simply, we may say that the death of Cordelia is totally and horrifyingly unnecessary, a gratuitous twisting of *ath of Cordelia robs "hero of tragic illumination."

the knife in the wound. It is not needed to resolve any knotty
tangle of the plot. It is countermanded by the very man who
ordered it in the first place, nor has the audience any reason to
believe that it will take place. Above all, it not only teaches Lear
nothing but rather topples him swiftly from the heights of tragic
tranquillity to something like the frenzied ravings of the storm
scenes.

Thus the death of Cordelia subverts almost all our expectations of tragedy. It robs the hero of tragic illumination and his
suffering of 'educative' or redemptive power. It casts the
shadow of an enormous question mark on the conception of
tragedy as an affirmation of life against evil and suffering, and
with it on the existence of any intelligible moral order. Finally,
as we have seen in another context, it makes it impossible for
the survivors to give a convincing and true account of the tragic
hero's achievement. In all these ways, we can see that *King Lear*
includes and transcends, and by transcending raises doubts
about, the claims of tragedy to be a true and ennobling report
on human life.

If we ask ourselves what the purpose of such a radical
subversion of the consolations of tragedy is, the best answer we
can come up with may be that the very pointlessness of
Cordelia's death and Lear's suffering is their point. In other
words, *King Lear* compels us to face the obvious but too often
ignored fact that tragedy, like all artistic genres, is a human
construct and has no necessary transcendental guarantee
behind it. Reality may not endorse the nobleness and worth of
suffering in the same unequivocal way that tragedy does. This
is perhaps why *King Lear* has been *the* Shakespearean tragedy of
our time for audience, directors and critics alike – for in our
time, too, the heroic claims of tragedy speak less compellingly
than the narrower, shriller and more subdued tones of the
grotesque.

4 THE THEATRICAL RHYTHM

To many of us the plot of *King Lear* is so familiar that we may
not realise, as the first audience must have done, how full of

dramatic surprises the play is. In the great final scene for
instance, as already indicated, a first-time audience would not
know that Cordelia was to die, especially if it was familiar with
the old *Leir* play. Indeed, it may expect the main plot to
contrast with the sub-plot, and Lear's fate to be substantially
different from Gloucester's. After all, we have all the forces of
evil displayed dead or dying on stage, except Cornwall who has
died earlier. Even when the stage direction says '*Enter a
Gentleman with a bloody knife*', we are uncertain for a while who
has been killed, till the bodies of the two sisters are brought in.
Then there is the desperate urgency of Edmund's counter-
manding order to the Officer, brought to nothing by the
poignant entry of Lear bearing Cordelia in his arms.

This is the dramatic rhythm of *King Lear*: a pattern of
expectations deliberately aroused and systematically frus-
trated. We can see it in particular details as well as in the larger
design of the play. It is set in motion at the very beginning,
when the topics of the brief conversation between Gloucester
and Kent – the king's decision to divide the kingdom and the
coming home of Gloucester's illegitimate son – might lead us to
think that the play to follow was a political drama or perhaps a
sexual comedy rather than one of the bleakest of tragedies. At
the very end we have the stunning irony of Albany's line 'The
gods defend her' (Cordelia) immediately preceding the
momentous stage direction '*Enter Lear with Cordelia in his arms*'.
In the vast and various drama which intervenes, there are
many more instances of hopes and expectations which are
aroused only to be thwarted. The alert reader/spectator/
auditor who approaches the play as far as possible as if it was
new to him will find many examples for himself. Here there is
room to indicate only a few of the most important.

An instance of unfulfilled expectation on a larger scale may
be found in the phase of the drama which follows the blinding of
Gloucester. The scene, precisely because it is so horrible,
suggests that the worst may be over. A servant has died trying
to protect the old man and killed his torturer, another binds his
wounds and leads him towards friendly help. It looks as if the
forces of justice and compassion are rousing themselves. Yet
the relief is only temporary, for it leads Gloucester to his
nightmare encounter with the mad king. Earlier we have seen

how Kent's good wishes to Gloucester – 'the gods reward your kindness!' [III vi 5] – are followed by the latter's blinding in the very next scene. Gloucester's 'Grace go with you, Sir!' to Edgar precedes the latter's immediate return with 'Away, old man! . . . King Lear hath lost' [v ii 5–6]. And each of Edgar's optimistic comments is ironically highlighted by a worsening of the situation till he himself is forced to conclude that events are too overwhelming for the comfort of moralising: 'I would not take this from report. It is; / And my heart breaks at it' (though it doesn't take Edgar long to revert to his bad habit [see v iii 168–71]).

The frustration of our hopes at every turn is not merely a dramatic device to wring as much suspense out of the action as possible. It is profoundly true to the tragic insight which informs the play: namely, that human cruelty and the vagaries of chance can exceed our worst forebodings.

One of the many ways in which Shakespeare shows his increasing mastery of his art is in the confidence and virtuosity with which he uses the resources of the Jacobean playhouse. Nowhere is this better seen than in the construction of *King Lear*. A brief discussion of two characteristic scenes will serve to bring this out clearly. I have chosen the storm scenes in Act III and Gloucester's attempted suicide [VI vi].

(a) Act III. Harley Granville-Barker rightly remarked that the most important element in Shakespeare's stagecraft was the word. In a theatre without painted scenery or artificial light, most effects of locality, time and atmosphere had to be created through language. We can see how triumphantly this is achieved in the storm scenes. Ironically (as we shall see in Part Two), this very fact has created problems when the play has been staged in later theatres, where elaborate devices for the creation of rain, wind and thunder effects have often interfered with the delivery of the words themselves or made them seem redundant.

The sound of the storm is first heard while Lear is still indoors [II iv 279]; and, before we see Lear himself, an anonymous Gentleman gives Kent a vivid account of the distraught king which not only evokes the storm but associates it with the tempest raging in Lear's mind:

> Contending with the fretful elements:
> Bids the wind blow the earth into the sea,
> Or swell the curléd waters 'bove the main,
> That things might change or cease; tears his white hair,
> Which the impetuous blasts with eyeless rage
> Catch in their fury and make nothing of;
> Strives in his little world of man to out-storm
> The to-and-fro conflicting wind and rain.   [III i 4–11]

The very anonymity of the utterance gives it an impersonal choric force, so that when Lear himself begins to utter his violent imprecations [ii 1–9 & 14–24] it is as if he has borrowed the voice of the tempest. His changing attitude to the elements is an important stage in his 'redemption'. He sees them first as agents of universal destruction, then as instruments of divine justice and finally as the means by which he can struggle out of self-pity into pity for the wretched of the earth. Almost as important as the language through which this widening of vision occurs is the physical movement that seems to be called for as its accompaniment. Kent makes four separate attempts to persuade Lear to come indoors and each time Lear evades him, claiming that his mental sufferings make the storm seem nothing and finally telling Kent to seek shelter himself. The effect is to isolate Lear on the stage. When he begins to feel pity for the 'poor naked wretches' he is separated from the others (an effect more noticeable on the 'thrust' stage of the Jacobean playhouse than on a modern proscenium-arch stage), and this isolation is heightened when he confronts Poor Tom and resolves to 'unbutton here'. When he takes Tom's arm and separates himself from the others, the action signals the advent of his madness.

We should realise that not only the anonymous Gentleman and Lear himself but all the characters involved help to 'create' the storm on stage through the apparently confused but really carefully orchestrated diffusing of their lines. Thus through word and movement the storm scenes come alive as both a violent upheaval in the world outside and a chaos leading to madness in 'the little world' of Lear's mind.

(b) *Act* IV, *sc.* vi. The 'Dover cliff' scene is perhaps the most brilliant piece of sheer theatrical virtuosity in all Shakespeare's plays. It is inextricably bound up with the particular stage for which it was written and cannot be successfully realised except in terms of the conventions of that stage.

To begin with, even before we arrive at Dover we are apprehensive that Gloucester, having escaped death at his torturer's hands, really will commit suicide; only at the very end do we experience the accustomed reversal of expectation. Secondly, when we do arrive, we are never quite certain where we are. On a stage with visual indications of place, locations are invariably 'painted' by a character's words. But here Edgar is an 'unreliable commentator'; in fooling Gloucester he may also be fooling us, which adds to our sense of bewilderment. At first, when Gloucester feels the ground as even and Edgar insists that it is steep and asks his father if he hears the sea, it is as if Shakespeare were deliberately playing with the principal means by which place was signified in his theatre. Edgar's speech [IV vi 11–24] so powerfully evokes a non-existent but vertiginously 'real' landscape that, especially in its Jacobean setting, the impression of an actual place must have been all but irresistible. Within the scene Edgar must play two quite distinct roles and in a single line (when the king enters) speak in his 'own' voice. The 'actual' suicide of Gloucester pushes the imaginative powers of the audience to their very limit, for all that has 'really' happened is that an actor has fallen flat on a level stage, yet we must experience it with Gloucester as a 'miracle' while at the same time perceiving how the miracle was worked and therefore withholding our assent from Edgar's confident optimism ('Bear free and patient thoughts').

By such means Shakespeare turns limitations into opportunities and harnesses the resources of his stage to the service of his dramatic vision.

5   Dramatic Structure and Style

Only an attentive reading of the whole play or a thoughtful production could illustrate the astonishing range of styles which Shakespeare orchestrated in *King Lear*. But we may sample some of this variety by considering two extracts from the extreme ends, so to speak, of the play's rhetorical scale: Edmund's 'Thou, Nature, art my goddess' soliloquy, and the 'trial' scene.

(a) *Act* I, *sc.* ii. Edmund's speech at the beginning of this scene has a smoothness and firm logical structure which are the exception rather than the rule in this play. The actor alive to the possibilities of the role will make good use of the contrast between the courteous and deferential son of the first scene and the confident and calculating imposter of this speech. He would give 'Nature' the weight demanded by the sense both at the beginning and when he repeats the words a few lines later, bearing in mind the way in which Edmund's conception of 'Nature' collides with other views throughout the tragedy. The series of questions into which he launches almost immediately is intended partly to establish a rapport with the audience; but the obsessive repetition of 'bastard', 'base' and related terms suggests a deep-going inner itch, a defensive guilt which occasions his eloquent protest but which somehow survives it at a level below that of rational argument. In other words, Edmund is here engaged in convincing himself as much as in persuading the audience, and the lines are nicely poised between audience address and introspection. There is real passion mixed with the contempt in phrases such as 'more composition and fierce quality' and 'Got between sleep and wake'. From here, at 'Well then' the rhythm is more relaxed for a moment, though 'legitimate' again sets off a mine of suppressed resentment. By the time he reaches the end of the speech Edmund is able to repeat the key words 'base' and 'bastards' with a much more cheerful air, so that the last line sounds like an exultant battle cry: which is what it is.

At the close we have a strong sense of sympathy with a young man who is eloquent and witty and genuinely wronged, and are prepared to take a keen interest in his future activities. Any moral reservations we may have at this point are fairly weak compared with the favourable impression created here of confident and purposeful energy and active intelligence.

(b) *Act* III, *sc.* vi. More typical of the staple idiom of *King Lear* than the kind of deliberate and formally structured utterance just discussed – especially in the latter part of the play when the conventions and assumptions which give it authority crumble under the pressure of disastrous experience – is the strange and haunting language of the 'trial' scene [lines 6ff.]. Granville-Barker aptly summarises the general quality of this scene:

> The lunatic mummery of the trial comes near to something we might call pure drama – as one speaks of pure mathematics or pure music – since it cannot be rendered into other terms than its own. Its effect depends upon the combination of the sound and meaning of the words and the sight of it being brought to bear as a whole directly upon our sensibility.
>
> (*Prefaces to Shakespeare*, vol. 1 [1972 edn] p. 294)

As this comment implies, it is impossible to discuss the dialogue of the different speakers in isolation. We note how the pretended ravings of Poor Tom are counterpointed by the near-hysterical riddling of the Fool which in turn links up with the shrill outbursts of the mad king. There are a few intelligible links between the speakers; for instance, Edgar's 'Pray, innocent' seems to be addressed to the Fool, who in turn passes the conversational ball to Lear with his riddle. But the real connections in the scene by-pass rational or logical continuity in favour of associations of theme and mood – thus, the first few lines play on the theme of demonic possession and the torments of hell as a punishment for the wrong-doer. This helps to fix Lear's crazed consciousness obsessively on the idea of trial and subsequent punishment for those who have wronged him: 'I will arraign them straight.' Perhaps it is the Fool's earlier reference to animals which sparks off Lear's 'No, you she-foxes'. Edgar may be referring either to the king or to the imagined demon with whom he is much concerned when he says, 'Look where he stands and glares!' The actor concerned will speak the line differently according to the choice he makes. The puzzling question, 'Want'st thou eyes at trial, madam?', adds to the general vocabulary of eyesight and blindness; Edgar may be asking 'Goneril' or 'Regan' to take notice of the fiend (or the king) looking at her. The atmosphere of irrationality is heightened by the snatch of popular ballad with its veiled hint of obscenity and the reference to the belly and 'croak' (meaning 'rumble' as applied to a stomach) is an instance of the way in which the play's language, even in its wildest flights, keeps in touch with the humdrum realities of human existence.

Lear's address to Edgar as 'thou robed man of justice' is a bizarre reference to the blanket in which Poor Tom is wrapped, and the formality of the address to both Edgar and Kent highlights the element of grotesque parody. The second scrap of song has to do with neglect of duty, no doubt negatively suggested to Edgar by 'Let us deal justly', while the harsh physical reality of 'She kicked the poor king her father' would take the audience's mind back to the real injury done by Goneril to Lear even while it recognises its literal inaccuracy. The Fool's unexpected words, 'Cry you mercy, I took you for a joint-stool' (also a form of insulting apology for not noticing someone), is a daring dramatic stroke, bringing to our attention the actuality of what we see, yet defying us to believe that that is all there is to the scene. Lear's four ensuing lines have a demented logic of their own, with their harping on the twin ideas of the wrong-doer escaping, and of the corruption of justice. The increasing strain on Edgar, who acts here also as a kind of recorder of the audience's reaction, shows itself in his exclamation and aside. Poor Tom's doggerel then transforms the touching poignancy of Lear's 'the little dogs and all' into something far grimmer. At the end of the 'trial' Lear's sudden and new-found but precariously held coherence – beginning 'Then let them anatomise Regan' – is all the more striking for arising out of the wild utterances which precede it and relapsing into them.

The whole scene is, of course, intended to contrast visually and thematically with the opening one in which Lear in his regal sanity dispensed absolute justice. To quote Granville-Barker again: 'Was better justice done, the picture ironically asks, when he presided in majesty and sanity and power?'

PART TWO: PERFORMANCE

6 INTRODUCTION

The following four productions have been chosen, among many, for description and comparison, as contributing most usefully, in my opinion, to our understanding of key themes in *King Lear* and of possibilities in staging and in the interpretation of character.

1. The Old Vic production of 1940 (Lewis Casson/Harley Granville-Barker); *Lear* John Gielgud; *Cordelia* Jessica Tandy; *Goneril* Cathleen Nesbitt; *Regan* Fay Compton; *Fool* Stephen Haggard; *Edmund* Jack Hawkins; *Edgar* Robert Harris; *Gloucester* Nicholas Hannen. Designer: Roger Furse.

2. The Stratford-upon-Avon and London RSC production of 1962 (Peter Brook); *Lear* Paul Scofield; *Cordelia* Diana Rigg; *Goneril* Irene Worth; *Regan* Patience Collier; *Fool* Alec McGowan; *Edmund* James Booth; *Edgar* Brian Murray; *Gloucester* Alan Webb. Designer: Peter Brook.

3. The RSC production of 1968 (Trevor Nunn); *Lear* Eric Porter; *Cordelia* Diane Fletcher; *Goneril* Sheila Allen; *Regan* Susan Fleetwood; *Fool* Michael Williams; *Edmund* Norman Rodway; *Edgar* Alan Howard; *Gloucester* Sebastian Shaw. Designer: Christopher Morley.

4. The Russian film version of 1970 (Grigori Kozintsev); *Lear* Yuri Yarvet; *Cordelia* Valentina Shendrikova; *Goneril* Elsa Radzinya; *Regan* Galina Volchek; *Fool* Oleg Dal; *Edmund* Regimastas Adomaitis; *Edgar* Leonard Merzin; *Gloucester* K. Cebric. Designer: Eduard Vanuntz.

As most readers will not have seen the three stage productions or even the film, I shall begin with a brief account of each before going on to comment in detail on some important features of the play – features discussed in Part One from a different angle or, rather, with a different emphasis – as they are interpreted in the productions concerned.

Casson/Granville-Barker Production, Old Vic, 1940

This, the earliest of the stage interpretations chosen for examination, is the only one I have not seen myself. Though compelled, therefore, to rely on others for my knowledge of it, I include it for a number of reasons. In the first place, an interpretation of the title role by Sir John Gielgud – whom many consider the greatest Shakespearean actor of his generation – demands attention. Secondly, although the production was officially credited to Lewis Casson, the programme note indicated that it was 'based upon Harley Granville-Barker's Preface to *King Lear* and his personal advice besides'. Granville-Barker was one of those rare figures who spoke with equal authority as a theatrical and a literary critic, and his *Prefaces* have been and are widely influential. This was the first Shakespearean production he had personally supervised. Finally, as we shall see, this production marked the high point of a particular conception of the play, a conception which we may for the moment call 'heroic naturalism'.

Visually, this production anchored the tragedy firmly not so much to the supposed period of the play – pre-Christian Britain – as to the actual period of its writing: Europe in the age of absolute monarchy. The costumes were mainly of elegantly cut satin and well-trimmed fur; coiffures and beards were carefully styled, and elaborate jewellery, footwear and accessories much in evidence. 'The stage', we are told, 'blazed colour, but with darkness beyond' (Audrey Williamson, *Old Vic Drama*, 1953). Lear's throne was impressive in the manner of a Renaissance monarch's, and the various castle interiors constructed with style and dignity in the setting designed by Roger Furse. The storm scenes were rendered with some degree of realism in sound and visual effects. But true to Granville-Barker's injunction in his Preface to the play that the unity and rhythm of the play should not be checked by the need for elaborate scene-changes, indications of different locales were achieved chiefly by swift changes in the multi-levelled set.

The style of acting seems to have been naturalistic, too, though embracing formality at one extreme and intimacy, pathos and the chaos of madness at the other: a chaos, which like all memorable theatrical effects (except lucky accidents),

1. Jack Hawkins as the plausible Renaissance courtier and Fay Compton as Regan in the Casson/Granville-Barker production, Old Vic, 1940. © Angus McBean, photograph, Harvard Theatre Collection.

2. The aftermath of Lear's rage against his elder daughter in Peter Brook's production, RSC, 1962, with Albany (Peter Jeffrey) and Goneril (Irene Worth). © Angus McBean, courtesy of the Shakespeare Centre.

3. Edgar leading the blind Gloucester in Peter Brook's production, RSC, 1962, with Edgar/Poor Tom (Brian Murray), Gloucester (Alan Webb) and Oswald (Clive Swift). © Angus McBean, courtesy of the Shakespeare Centre.

4. Power's pyramid before its collapse in Trevor Nunn's production, RSC, 1968. *Left to right:* Cornwall (Patrick Stewart), Regan (Susan Fleetwood), Goneril (Sheila Allen), Lear (Eric Porter) and Cordelia (Diane Fletcher). © *Birmingham Post and Mail.*

5. The 1970 Russian film version with Lear (Yuri Yarvet), Gloucester (K. Cebric) and Edgar (Leonard Merzin), directed by Grigori Kozintsev. © Contemporary Films Ltd, London.

6. The Kozintsev 1970 Russian film version with Lear (Yuri Yarvet) and Cordelia (Valentina Shendrikova). © Contemporary Films Ltd, London.

was the result of intense concentration and self-discipline. We learn, too, that the actors, especially the principal player, were not afraid of grand effects such as centre-stage exits and entrances, sweeping, larger-than-life gestures, and a deliberately 'rhetorical' use of voice. According to Gielgud's own reminiscences (*Stage Directions*, 1963), Granville-Barker's 'first concern was certainly for the speaking of the verse and the balance of the voices'. Fortunately, Gielgud includes in his book the verbatim notes which he took down during Granville-Barker's rehearsals, from which we can get some idea of the careful thought and imaginative attention which went into the realisation of a particular effect in voice or gesture.

Peter Brook's Production, RSC, Stratford and London, 1962

Perhaps no interpretation of *King Lear* in our time has been more talked about than this one, launched at the Memorial Theatre and later brought to London, with Paul Scofield as Lear and Alec McGowan as the Fool. This is Brook's first and (so far) only production of the play, for which he himself designed the setting. It consisted mainly of a bare stage with two enormous off-white 'flats' on each side and a sort of rough fence lowered to suggest a building or barricade. Necessary stage furnishings such as tables and chairs were roughly fashioned of wood or twisted metal, and the costumes (of no particular historical period) were of leather treated to suggest age and use. For the storm scenes three large vibrating metal sheets were lowered from the 'flies'. The lighting was intensely bright and scarcely altered throughout the performance.

The entire conception and production, as Brook himself acknowledged, was greatly influenced by a controversial critical study ('*King Lear*, or Endgame') by the Polish critic Jan Kott, subsequently published (1964) in the English version of his general critique, *Shakespeare Our Contemporary*. Where the Casson/Barker/Gielgud production was full of colour and splendour, the Brook/Scofield interpretation was deliberately drab and muted; and where the earlier one was specifically located in a historical period, the later one was indeterminate in both space and time. Some of the implications of these and other differences will be touched on below. For the time being we may note that, to judge by the volume of critical and popular interest it aroused, the Brook/Scofield *Lear* undoubtedly struck a responsive chord in the theatre-going public of the early 1960s, as the Casson/Barker/Gielgud one did in the very different theatre-going public of 1940. Again, we are fortunate in having what amounts to a detailed record of the rehearsals for this production and the thinking behind it, written by Charles Marowitz who assisted Brook with the production and published as *Lear Log* (1963).

Trevor Nunn's Production, RSC, 1968

According to Irving Wardle, the theatre critic of *The Times*, the Royal Shakespeare Company's 1968 production of *King Lear* did not quite escape 'the shadow of the Brook/Scofield *Lear*' done by the same company six years earlier. The bare stage of the earlier production was here relieved with costumes of gold net and crowns of barbaric beauty. The scene of Lear's first entry was especially impressive, with the king brought on within an enormous tent carried by attendants with blazing torches and occupying most of the down-stage area. When the front of the tent is opened, we see Lear on his throne with the Fool crouched at his feet. The physical closeness of Lear and the Fool was a marked feature of this production.

Many changes of lighting were used to suggest mood, time and location, in contrast to the unchanging baleful brightness of the Brook/Scofield production. Costumes and properties carried a more definite, though still vague, suggestion of a historical period, pagan Britain. Again, the storm scenes attempted some realism, especially in the sound effects. Most critics found Eric Porter's Lear solid and intelligent but not quite grand enough in stature in the high moments of the tragedy. Their judgement may have been coloured by the fact that Porter took on the title role soon after playing the part of the cold and successful businessman Soames Forsyte in the enormously popular TV serial *The Forsyte Saga*.

One personal memory of this production may be added to

emphasise that critical judgements on theatrical performances are based, not on something comparatively stable like a dramatic text, but on what is always different each time. Many critics praised the final entrance of King Lear with the dead Cordelia in his arms in this production for its simple and heart-rending pathos. On the night I saw the play, however, the effect was somewhat marred because Eric Porter (due to injury, perhaps) did not carry the dead Cordelia himself, but came forward with two soldiers bearing Cordelia, fully armed, at his side.

Grigori Kozintsev's Russian Film Version, 1970

Kozintsev based his production on Boris Pasternak's translation of the play, with music specially composed by Dimitri Shostakovich. This is the finest film version of any Shakespeare play I have ever seen, in that it captured in cinematic terms the energy and magnitude of Shakespeare's vision without sacrificing its moments of intimacy and haunting pathos. Kozintsev has written that 'the process of tracing the spiritual life of Shakespeare's plays cannot be separated from the tracing of the historical process' ('*Hamlet* and *King Lear*: Stage and Film', in *Shakespeare 1971*, ed. C. Leech and J. Margeson [1972]), and the film attempts to project the one through the other. A historical period is suggested by the long flowing robes of the principal characters; and the pikes and helmets of the soldiers, who figure prominently in the action, may indicate that it is late Renaissance.

What is far more striking than the sense of a particular time, however, is the vivid realisation of place. By this I do not mean that the film specifies the country or city where the action takes place, but rather that it gives us a vivid cumulative impression of the physical presence of the landscape: something which the cinema by its very nature is well equipped to do. We are made fully aware of Lear as an autocratic monarch who rules a bare and inhospitable land without much knowledge of or interest in its inhabitants – mainly a seemingly endless procession of 'poor naked wretches', as the opening shot of the halt, the blind, the sick and the hungry shows us. The basic rhythm of the film is achieved by a beautifully balanced alternation between long and medium shots of this peopled landscape and startlingly vivid close-ups of the central characters. Another striking effect is the appearance of King Lear himself (Yuri Yarvet): not, as we might expect, a physically substantial and robust old man, but a wispy, white-haired figure whose strength of passion surprises us.

The scene of Gloucester's blinding is eliminated and the sub-plot and main plot are brought closer together by a skilful juxtaposition of scenes. Music is used to great dramatic effect, especially in the haunting flute melody played by the Fool: a wide-eyed, bald-headed figure who, for all that he appears to be a congenital idiot in the clinical sense, seems touched with a kind of prophetic power.

These brief descriptions, together with the illustrations, will serve to give the reader some idea of the distinctive qualities of each interpretation of the tragedy and make, I hope, the following discussion of particular aspects clear and helpful.

7   SETTING AND COSTUMES: HISTORY V. UNIVERSALITY

Every Shakespeare play presents the director and designer with a problem at the very outset, that of visual realisation. Should *Macbeth* be played against an eleventh-century Scottish background, with an approximation to the rough cloaks and kilts of the period (as Orson Welles chose to do in his ill-advised film)? Or should it be staged in Jacobean settings and costumes, even in modern ones, or in an eclectic mixture of all these? Shakespeare's own theatre seems to have favoured something like the latter solution – using, for instance, a combination of togas and doublets for *Titus Andronicus*, if we are to rely on the evidence of a rough sketch which has survived from the period.

King Lear presents the problem in a particularly acute form. Throughout the nineteenth century there was an increasing emphasis on realistic visual and aural effects (facilitated by the development of sophisticated stage machinery), and a striving for as great a degree of historical and archaeological accuracy as possible. A reviewer of Macready's pioneering 1838 production, with Shakespeare's text and the Fool restored after a century and a half of thralldom to Tate's travesty, found that the setting

> corresponds with the period and with the circumstances of the text. The castles are heavy, sombre, solid; their halls adorned with trophies of the chase and instruments of war; druid circles rise in spectral loneliness out of the heath, and the 'dreadful pother' of the elements is kept up with a verisimilitude which beggars all that we have hitherto seen attempted. Forked lightnings, now vividly illuming the broad horizon, now faintly coruscating in small and serpent folds, play in the distance; the sheeted element sweeps over the foreground, and then leaves it in pitchy darkness; and wind and rain howl and rush in 'tyranny of the open night'.
>
> (*John Bull*, 28 January 1808; quoted by Maynard Mack in *'King Lear' in Our Time* [1965].)

The picture-frame stage encouraged the depiction of realistic scenes, and the verbal power and music of the storm scenes, for example, was often sacrificed to spectacular visual and aural effects which rendered the words almost redundant. Furthermore, the antiquarian interest which was widespread throughout the nineteenth century led actor-managers and their scenic designers to make definite and local what is often, for good reasons, not specified in the text itself. Thus, Charles Kean's vision of *King Lear* saw the action as taking place in eighth-century Anglo-Saxon England, while Irving placed it in a period just after the Romans had left Britain. Whatever the historical period chosen, the price paid for such verisimilitude was always the same: the frequent rearrangement and drastic mutilation of scenes to suit the need for elaborate scene changes, and the consequent distortion or destruction of the play's poetic power and dramatic rhythm.

In reaction to this misconception and maltreatment of Shakespeare, The Elizabethan Stage Society, founded in 1895 by William Poel, attempted to return to the fluidity and simplicity of Shakespeare's own stage. Harley Granville-Barker, who shared Poel's approach and had, by all accounts, a much keener sense of theatre, is particularly caustic in his Preface to *King Lear* on the damage done to the play's essential

structure and rhythm by too much preoccupation with specific-
ity of setting. It was Poel's original conception of Edmund as a
typically Machiavellian Renaissance nobleman which
Granville-Barker developed in the Old Vic *Lear* of 1940. Here
the splendour and elegance of a Renaissance court was the
effect aimed at, and 'the great image of authority' with which
the action opens was firmly placed in the playwright's own
time.

By way of contrast, the setting and costumes of Trevor
Nunn's 1968 production (designed by Christopher Morley)
were much less historically determined. The basic contrast in
costume lay in the gleam of gold and the drabness of rags, and
the shapes of crowns and cloaks suggested (without specifying)
a barbaric period of the pagan past. Ronald Bryden, the
Observer's theatre critic, described the setting as 'a legendary
limbo, a fairy-tale world of sombrely magnificent gold and furs
flickering into torchlit life out of prehistoric blackness'. The
reference to legend and fairy-tale suggests part of the impulse
behind such a production: namely, to bring out the element of
myth or folklore which is undoubtedly present in the play and
which has seemed to modern directors (influenced perhaps by
Freudian and other ideas about the symbolic significance of
folklore motifs) more central than the purely historical one.
Where pomp and authority were identified in the 1940
production with Renaissance absolutism, Trevor Nunn's production found a less historically specific but enormously
powerful theatrical image for it in the great entry of Lear in his
covered tent gleaming against the darkness in the fitful light of
flares.

Peter Brook's solution in 1962 to the problem of settings and
costume may be approached by way of an earlier production
which had much the same view of the visual dimension but was
generally acknowledged to have failed entirely to achieve it on
the stage. This – fifteen years after the Old Vic interpretation,
with Gielgud as Lear – was the 1955 production by and with
him, with settings and costumes by the Japanese-American
artist Isamu Noguchi. The aims of the production as set out in
Gielgud's producer's note in the programme were admirable.
They were:

... to find a setting and costumes which would be free of historical or decorative association so that the timeless, universal and mythical quality of the story may be clear. We have tried to present the play and characters in a very simple and basic manner for the play to come to life in the words and the acting.

The result, unfortunately, fell well below expectations, and Gielgud himself described the production as 'little short of disastrous'. Noguchi's notion of 'a very simple and basic manner' consisted of abstract geometrical shapes in primary colours for settings, and, as far as the human anatomy permitted, for costumes. These were based on an elaborate symbolism of shape and colour which apparently did not communicate itself as part of the audience's theatrical experience. (Some idea of the visual effect of this 1955 production may be gained from the Folio Society edition of *King Lear* which reproduces in colour Noguchi's designs, with explanatory notes.)

Peter Brook shared Gielgud's aims of avoiding historical particularity and aspired towards the visual equivalent of timeless universality, but his inspiration was translated to the stage in radically different terms. Kozintsev recalls (in *The Space of Tragedy*, p. 95) receiving a letter from Brook in which the latter 'wrote amusingly that directors who produce Shakespeare with realistic scenery, faithfully reproducing historical details, are behaving dishonestly and cheating their audience until they begin to believe that in "historical times" people did not talk naturally to each other but in this strange way (as in Shakespeare's poetry)'.

No one could accuse the 1962 Brook/Scofield production of any interest in reproducing historical details, faithfully or otherwise. The main setting, as has been noted, consisted of two enormous uncoloured 'flats' with rusty and indeterminate metal shapes placed against them. The furniture and accessories were rough-hewn and gave the appearance of decay. The storm was created by Lear's words and actions, aided only by the vibration of metal screens suspended from the 'flies', no music being used here or elsewhere in the production. (By contrast, several critics of Trevor Nunn's 1968 production found that the musical and sound effects interfered with the words in the storm scenes.) Kozintsev, who saw the Brook/ Scofield production during its Russian tour, gives us a vivid description, not only of the visual effect —

> The bareness of the evenly lit stage, plain sackcloth, a few pieces of iron, the leather costumes (reminding one of decayed sheepskins dug up by archaeologists from an ancient burial ground) enclosed the action of the tragedy in a cold and timeless emptiness. It was as if all the clocks in the world had stopped.

— but also of the image in the tragedy which Brook had seen as central and which inspired his setting:

> Brook evidently gave the greatest significance to Kent's last speech. . . . In an emptiness where there is iron, rotting leather, corpses — Peter Brook wanted to create an image of the 'rack of this tough world' in all the magnificence of scenic desolation, in the greatness of the span of centuries (millennia?).
>
> (*The Space of Tragedy*, p. 23)

If we were to ask where the action of the play takes place, the only possible answer is: on the stage. Similarly, no answer is possible to the question: exactly when does all this happen? except 'during the performance'. If as theatre-goers we feel somewhat cheated by such answers, it is perhaps because we do not habitually or seriously question the validity of the idea that every play must be imagined as taking place somewhere or at some time. Much modern drama and fiction has questioned this assumption, notably the plays of Samuel Beckett. It is no accident that Brook has acknowledged Beckett's influence on his view of theatre in general and *King Lear* in particular. (As we have earlier noted, Jan Kott's essay on the play, acknowledged by Brook as a major influence, makes explicit reference to a Beckett play in its title: '*King Lear*, or Endgame'). Brook found no anachronism in seeing Shakespeare in Beckettian terms, since he believes (almost certainly correctly) that Beckett's own plays have been deeply marked by the vision and dramatic technique of *King Lear*.

One of the dangers of aspiring to universality and timelessness is that no visual image, however abstract, is entirely 'free of historical or decorative association', just as no garment is entirely without a suggestion of period. If you are careless or imprudent or just unlucky, you might end up reminding your audience, not of universal symbolism and timeless values, but of *inappropriate* visual images and historical or social situations. As was demonstrated by some of the Noguchi costumes for Gielgud's 1955 production, a triangular shape may be intended to symbolise the dominance of personal will, but to many people a man clad in one would look like a walking tent. In the same way, though the costumes and furniture in Brook's production were intended to give a general unlocalised impression of universal decay, they did not succeed in doing so for everyone. One critic was reminded by Lear's hunting outfit of 'a motor-cyclist's leather jacket with gauntlets and a pair of gumboots', and another described an item of stage furniture as 'a buckled mudguard which threatened to castrate several actors who sat on it'. Such occasional misapprehensions are unavoidable and perhaps tell us as much about the critic as about the performance. Generally, however, the Brook/Scofield *Lear* is held to have succeeded in the effect it aimed for: of a timeless tragedy about the inescapable human condition which was both its theme and its setting.

Since, as we have seen, Grigori Kozintsev believes in the inseparability of the 'spiritual' and 'historical' processes in Shakespeare's plays, the problem posed by the 1970 film was not that of avoiding any historical reference but of making such reference universal in its applicability. 'The essence of the art of film-making', he has said in a lecture, 'consists in the linking of these two view points. The close shot catches the barely perceptible spiritual movement, while the general view shows the movement of historical time.' We see here an explanation for the alteration of close-up and mid- or long-shot which has earlier been noted as providing the rhythm of the film. But the question still remains: what are these shots to be of, what kind of landscape, buildings, clothes and so on are to be included within them?

In the lecture from which I have just quoted ('*King Lear*: Stage and Film'), Kozintsev makes the point that the Shakespearean world cannot be found either geographically or historically; nor can it be fabricated. It has to be patiently and sensitively inferred from the text itself, not so much as a set of clues pointing to a particular place or period, but rather as a series of indications of a tone, an atmosphere, a poetic world in which the life of the drama may be most fully realised. 'One has to seek out and decipher the poetic signs, the code. It is in the lines, and, as always happens with poetry, it's between the lines as well' (ibid.). Kozintsev found the code he was looking for predominantly in the speeches of Edgar as the mad Poor Tom and the world these speeches conjure up. Arguing that the speeches are excessive in quantity and dramatic force if their sole or main function was to assist Edgar's impersonation or hide him from his pursuers, the Russian director asserts that Poor Tom's world is the authentic voice of our world, the immediately recognisable link between extremity and violence in his day and ours. 'Here the world of tragedy is unfolded for us to see.' That world contains, as Kozintsev's vivid but always responsible imagination conceives and his film marvellously bodies forth, not only the bare and hostile landscape of suffering and need, but the dispossessed who pass by continually on it. 'There is nothing to eat and no shelter. Here, in the specific concreteness of life, lies the source of tragedy' (ibid.).

The film tries to suggest, not a particular historical period, but a stage in human social development, one where ties of family and tribe are fundamental and the 'family fireside a primary image'. Thus, the opening scene showed Lear not, as we might have expected, on a throne, but on a bench by his hearth – 'the ancient glow of the patriarchal fire'. And, in a manner very reminiscent of the development of dominant poetic metaphors throughout a Shakespeare play, this same fire is the key motif of the war scenes, which are shown, not as a series of set battle pieces, but as a running flame of violence: the visual symbol of suppressed personal, familial and tribal passions which literally consume the land.

8   Conceptions of Character and Relationships

Lear

Every director and actor has to begin where every reader does: with the text itself. But within the generous limits set by image and meaning, one director's view of the play will differ from another's – in much the same way that, though equally faithful to the score, one conductor's interpretation of a musical composition will differ from another's. We have seen how such differences of outlook and emphasis show themselves in varying visual presentations. They are similarly clearly marked in the depiction of character and relationships between characters. In this section I shall be looking at some of the distinctive features of the productions mentioned from this standpoint.

Like readers, directors and actors are inevitably influenced by notions of character which have been dominant in earlier theatrical, literary and pictorial tradition. For instance, the white-bearded, flowing-robed Blakean figure noted by Orwell as most readers' visual impression of Lear is a product of innumerable stage and pictorial portrayals of the tragic hero on these lines.

John Gielgud's interpretation of the title role in 1940 owed something to this tradition, for all that it was partly intended as a reaction against it. In referring earlier to Gielgud's interpretation I used the phrase 'heroic naturalism'. By this I meant to suggest that he appears to have played the king as a psychologically credible old man but one capable of a certain larger-than-life grandeur in the 'big' scenes. Gielgud records that the first time he read the part through with Granville-Barker in preparation for rehearsals, the latter remarked: 'Lear is an oak; you are an ash. We must see how this will serve you' (*Stage Directions*, p. 51). The thrust of the rehearsals was directed, as far as the title role was concerned, towards extracting an oak-like strength and solidity from an actor who, in grace of bearing, sinewy elegance of physique and melodiousness of voice, put Granville-Barker in mind of 'an ash'. The extent to which the sheer physical appearance and resources of an actor shape our conception of the character he portrays is often overlooked by theatre-goers, though it tends to be one of the first considerations of a director. Sheer physical bulk should not, of course, be confused with massive stage presence, though the actor who undertakes Lear needs considerable stamina. When Kozintsev deliberately chose a frail-looking actor as a contrast to the substantial 'Blakean' Lear of earlier convention, he took care to make his Gloucester a physically powerful figure as if to represent in him the old king's physical strength: a suggestion enhanced by the close links between the two plots effected by skilful cross-cutting.

Granville-Barker's conception of Lear was as a figure of 'megalithic grandeur', 'more a magnificent portent than a man' (*Prefaces*, p. 285), though Gielgud tells us that at the beginning of rehearsals the director made no attempt to force his views upon the actor, concentrating instead on the words themselves and the balance of voices. Nor did he have what Gielgud calls 'the modern fear of clichés in the acting of Shakespeare', encouraging, as we have noted, grand entrances, a declamatory style of speaking where this seemed appropriate, and expansive gestures: 'big' acting, to use stage jargon. The effect, in Gielgud's view, was 'classic, tragic, noble' – which he attributes to Granville-Barker's unerring theatrical sense and skill rather than to any exceptional ability on the actor's part. From the first impression of 'virile majesty', through the storm scenes seen as a 'contest with the elements', to the final stages with the death of Cordelia where Lear dies 'on a flare of hope more heart-rending than all the previous agony' (these phrases are taken from Audrey Williamson's eye-witness account) – this was clearly a portrayal cast in the heroic mould, affirming human dignity even in its destruction. Perhaps it is not altogether accidental that it was first staged in the dark days of 1940, on the eve of the fall of France. Its spirit seems to have been akin, for all the obvious differences between them, to another Shakespearean production of the time: Olivier's film of *Henry V*.

In extreme contrast, Paul Scofield's Lear in Peter Brook's 1962 production was almost totally devoid of classic dignity or heroic stature, as the terms are usually understood. As anyone who has seen the film *A Man for All Seasons* will know, Scofield is an actor who can, when called upon, convey human dignity and self-responsibility in the classic manner as powerfully as any actor of our time. The virtual absence of these qualities from his Lear was therefore clearly intentional. This was a Lear who wolfed his food in untidy handfuls, cackled unpleasantly at dirty jokes and overturned the furniture in his fits of temper. Whatever opinion they had of its faithfulness to Shakespeare's portrayal, most critics agreed that this Lear was a man, not an archetype, and a very earthy mortal at that. Even in appearance, the short greyish beard and close-cropped hair not only contrasted with the flowing white beard and locks of the traditional Lear but suggested an altogether more down-to-earth, smaller-scale figure. Neither in voice nor gesture did Scofield aspire to the range and expansiveness of Gielgud's Lear. Even in the storm scenes it could hardly be said that his voice created the storm, though it was certainly audible throughout (by no means the case even with all professional productions of these scenes). Much of the time, as when he sat with his clenched hands on the crude throne in the first scene, there was a stylised quality about his movements which invited the audience to observe and understand the man rather than to identify or sympathise with him. Clearly, this Lear was not a tragic hero in the accepted sense, but neither was the world he inhabited one where heroism or even tragedy were seen as possible. As Jan Kott remarks in the essay which largely inspired Peter Brook's production, the Lear world is one where the Book of Job is played by clowns. I shall return to the wider implications of these remarks and their theatrical realisation later.

Trevor Nunn's bare stage for the RSC in 1968 did not help Eric Porter to evoke much sympathy for Lear in the storm scenes, as it blurred the distinction between indoors and outdoors: a crucial one in a play where so much of the action consists of shutting people out or taking them into the human warmth of a dwelling. This Lear, with his flowing beard and shining bald head, looked not unlike the traditional figure. More than one critic was reminded of Tolstoy, especially as there was a generally Boyar-ish appearance in the soldiers' costumes, and thick furs were much in evidence. But when Lear stripped himself near-naked at 'Off, off, you lendings!', it was an awkward shock to notice the discrepancy between the ancient head and the lithe, youngish body. Though Porter seemed to play the king as a traditional tragic hero inviting sympathetic identification, many found his portrayal intelligent rather than moving: 'a Lear of solid merit but less than sublime', in the words that headlined *The Times* review.

Kozintsev's view of Lear challenged in its own terms the idea of the king as a Titan, a superman towering above his people.

This image is presented early on in the film, only to be quickly undermined both by the slight physique of the central figure and the numerous group shots which stress Lear's kinship with ordinary mortals and his existence as a necessary and inevitable product of this particular community. In Kozintsev's own words: 'Lear [is] seen first raised above the kneeling crowd and then seen as an old man from the "lower depths" of life, among the beggars from whose number he is barely distinguishable' (*Shakespeare 71*, p. 196).

The Fool and Cordelia

Next to Lear himself, these are undoubtedly the two most important characters in the tragedy – though it is somewhat misleading to talk about such an intricately inter-involved network of relationships in terms of the relative importance of separate characters. When Macready first restored the Fool in 1838, the part was played by a girl, and eyewitness accounts and illustrations clearly indicate that a kind of sentimental pathos was what was sought and achieved, rather than any close thematic link with the tragedy as a whole. 'A sort of fragile, hectic, beautiful-faced, half-idiot-looking boy', was how Macready himself phrased his conception, which Maynard Mack more succinctly summarises as 'a sort of feverish Peter Pan'. (His essay is reproduced in the Casebook on the play, pp. 62–3.) Many of the Fool's lines were omitted in the interests of both literary and social decorum (Macready prided himself on being a gentleman first and an actor chiefly by necessity). In modern times a much fuller and finer appreciation of the vital role of the Fool has been shown by critics and realised in many notable productions.

The main problem for the modern director and actor is that, though we are fully aware of the importance of the Fool in the play, we can no longer respond directly and intimately to 'the Fool', either as a familiar figure in aristocratic circles or as an equally familiar stock character on stage with a history going back to the Vice of the Medieval Morality drama (to say nothing for the moment of the 'natural' fool). If he is simply represented as a court jester complete with cap and bells, he is likely to come across as merely quaint and to produce the wrong kind of 'comic relief' (though I doubt whether Lear's Fool ever provides any sort of relief to the audience, any more than to Lear himself). Directors have therefore tried to find some kind of modern counterpart to the Fool or to remove him altogether from historical-social reality into the world of fantasy or nightmare.

The 1982 Stratford version of the Fool as circus clown (directed by Adrian Noble) was perhaps inspired by the visual metaphor of the circus which underpinned Peter Brook's famous production of *A Midsummer Night's Dream* in 1970, though here there seemed to be no such sustained visual framework to support it. Perhaps that was precisely the effect intended, that the Fool should appear totally out of place in this world. The general justification for playing the Fool as circus (or pantomime) clown is that the latter is still a fairly familiar figure and that he straddles the gap between the world of the play and the world of the audience.

There was still perhaps more than a trace of Macready's beautiful idiot in Stephen Haggard's playing of the role in the 1940 Gielgud production, to judge by Audrey Williamson's description of him as 'a strange frail creature with restless eyes, a cracked wandering song, an odd grotesque mixture of 'natural' and 'jester' (*Old Vic Drama*, p. 137).

As portrayed by Michael Williams in the 1968 Stratford production directed by Trevor Nunn, the Fool had two notable characteristics. First, he clung to Lear much of the time with almost literally dog-like tenacity and devotion, and secondly he was a creature more wild than pathetic, barely human and yet occasionally strangely Lear-like in gesture and appearance. There was clearly an attempt here to suggest that the master-servant relationship was not the only or the most important link between Lear and the Fool. The similarity between them, as well as their close proximity, prompted the feeling that the Fool was somehow a part of Lear's identity and consciousness (in the Russian film the Fool first appears from inside Lear's cloak): a part he strove desperately not to acknowledge yet one which suddenly welled up into his mind when he least expected it. The convulsive, almost involuntary spurts of speech and action which Michael Williams used conveyed this vividly, while the animal attitudes linked up with the imagery to underline the theme of man's kinship with the beasts which is part of Lear's vision of humanity at this point. At several moments too, one felt that it was not only Lear who was on the edge of madness but the Fool too, which once more reinforced the sense of identity between the two. Trevor Nunn's programme notes for this production suggest that one of the influences behind it was John Danby's critical study of the play – *Shakespeare's Doctrine of Nature* – and the portrayal of the Fool seemed to owe something to Danby's chapter on him: 'The Fool as Handy-Dandy'.

Alec McGowan, who played the fool to Scofield's Lear in Peter Brook's 1962 production, had a trace of the circus clown in the baggy pantaloons he wore, but this was a circus clown in the world of Beckett's Vladimir and Estragon: a 'bitter fool' indeed whose humour constantly showed the scars inflicted by a cruel and absurd world. During the storm scene he crouched by the side of the bare stage, fixing a long unwavering stare on the brightly lit arena, as if the sheer inexplicability of the universe in its dealings with man made any other response impossible. Suffering and the inacapacity to comprehend – that alone seemed to be all that existed in this world, pitilessly illuminated in every corner for our inspection. The rare moments in the performance when Lear seemed to evoke the audience's sympathy rather than its spell-bound fascination came almost entirely when King and Fool came together, as in Scofield's touching delivery of 'O fool, I shall go mad'.

The perception that the Fool is laughed at not because he is foolish or funny but because he speaks the truth lies at the heart of Kozintsev's view of the character. He recalls anecdotes about prison orchestras in Nazi concentration camps where the player-prisoners were beaten in order to make them play better. 'This', he writes, 'was the origin of the Fool-musician [in his film] – a boy taken from an orchestra composed of men condemned to death' (*Shakespeare 1971*, p. 198). He is no longer seen as a court comedian but as a poor urchin hovering indeterminately between youth and age, desperately telling the truth to people for whom 'nothing is funnier than the truth'. The thin, plaintive music of the Fool's pipe has an important function, marking first the feeble yet insistent presence of the

Fool himself and, when it rises over the requiem of the battle scenes, suggesting the indestructible tenacity of life simply going on: the still, sad music of humanity itself. For, unlike Brook's interpretation, Kozintsev's is haunted by the desperate yet unfailing belief in humanity's capacity to regenerate itself which he finds in the play. As he himself writes, *King Lear* is not only 'Theatre of Cruelty' but also 'Theatre of Mercy' (*Shakespeare 1971*, p. 197).

Cordelia's close relation to the Fool rests on more solid grounds than the supposition that the same boy-actor originally played both parts. Both are, in some important and unavoidable sense of the word, 'good' characters in an evil world to which they fall victim; both are touched with a kind of holy innocence yet they are both obstinately courageous, even foolhardy. Shakespeare's reference to the Fool pining away since Cordelia left for France [I iv 72–3] should not be overstressed, or sentimentalised; nevertheless it does point towards a special relationship between the two characters which productions often try to bring out, as in the opening of Adrian Noble's 1982 Stratford production. Since the Fool and Cordelia never meet, their kinship can usually be suggested on stage only by the one reminding us, by gesture, intonation and stage position, or a combination of these, of the other.

If she reminds us of the Fool, Cordelia should also remind us, especially at the beginning, of her father and his headstrong will. However much we may want to regard her as a purely symbolic figure, the presence of human actors on a stage inevitably recalls some family relationship when we are faced, for instance, with the direct collision of their wills:

LEAR   So young and so untender?
COR.   So young, my lord, and true.   [I i 107–8]

Not only their common strength of will but the fact that his youngest daughter is Lear's special favourite was emphasised by Gielgud when 'the voice melted to sweetness' as he turned slowly to Cordelia, (Williamson, p. 134: 1940 production), though the same critic found Jessica Tandy's Cordelia a little lacking in the paternal strength of will. Some indication of the kind and degree of attention Granville-Barker paid to the psychological motivation of Cordelia may be seen in his remark at rehearsal to Jessica Tandy: 'You are crying not because your father has been cruel, but because France has been kind' (Gielgud, *Stage Directions*, p. 122).

Trevor Nunn's 1968 production, doubtless influenced by Danby's view of Cordelia as a Christ-figure, saw her in fairly traditional symbolic terms as a saintly martyr in a wicked world. Diane Fletcher, who played the part, gave this conception a necessary substantiality by her commanding physical presence, aided by the fact that she was clad after her return from France like Joan of Arc in battle array. Although this may have detracted from the womanliness of Cordelia, it made the scene of her last meeting with her father extraordinarily touching. It had the disadvantage, however, of making Lear's final entry slightly awkward.

Diana Rigg played Cordelia in Peter Brook's 1962 production. Although, to quote one contemporary review, she behaved throughout 'like someone well able to take care of herself', the importance of her role was much diminished in Brook's interpretation of the play. By playing a sort of devil's advocate and inviting sympathy for Goneril and Regan, Brook reduced the emotional distance between them, making Cordelia almost an equal contender with the others. The scene of Lear's awakening and Cordelia's dialogue with him had little suggestion of a spiritual turning-point, being bleakly formal in setting and speech. Scofield's entry in a chair borne by attendants, rigid and statuesque with all human feeling carefully drained out, heightened the effect of detached presentation. At the very end of the play there was again a deliberate diminution of the significance of Cordelia's death in Scofield's response to it, which rather suggested that madness had returned some time before this final catastrophe. Edmund Gardner, writing in *Stage* (8 November 1962), went so far as to comment that 'no Lear has asked on such a brisk, cheerful note for a mirror to see whether Cordelia is dead'.

Kozintsev refers to Scofield's entry to meet Cordelia as 'a sort of blessed numbness'. His own realisation of Cordelia in the film was very different. For him a central moment in the play is the scene between Lear and Cordelia in captivity – 'goodness encircled by iron'. It is typical of his film's pervasive humanity that the camera does not simply dwell on Lear and Cordelia but shows other prisoners, their hands bound, walking silently past these two. Kozintsev also introduces (in accordance with his view of *Lear* as 'Theatre of Mercy' as well as of Cruelty) a scene where we are shown the marriage ceremony between the King of France and Cordelia. This takes place on a desolate beach well away from the royal precincts and represents an image of love and order rarely encountered in the tragedy that follows. Its relation to the king's own situation is emphasised by cross-cutting between Lear's procession and the shorter one at Cordelia's nuptials.

The Sisters, Gloucester and other Characters

There is space only for the briefest discussion of a few aspects of some of the other characters. While in some ways Goneril and Regan are, as I have suggested, like the wicked sisters of fairy-tale, directors and actresses have often sought to bring out certain differences in their characters. As Granville-Barker remarks, given the assumption that there are really wicked people in the world, they are as life-like as stage characters need to be and each develops freely in her own way. The same ingredients of outward reasonableness, hard-headed realism, an appetite for wanton cruelty and lust leading to mutual destruction occur in both characters, but in different proportions and with somewhat different effects.

Goneril is the more forthright character but Regan turns out to be the crueller, for it is she who insists on putting Gloucester's other eye out and savagely mocks him with the invitation to 'smell his way to Dover'. Regan's electrifying gesture with the hairpin in the 1982 Stratford production has been noted earlier (p. 26). Sexual appetite lies nearer the surface with Goneril (as Sheila Allen made effectively clear in Trevor Nunn's 1968 production), but once again, when it is roused in Regan, the younger sister is prepared to kill for it. In the same production Susan Fleetwood played Regan with a lady-like decorum combined with a girlish giggle in the blinding scene which suggested the 'undeveloped heart' from which such cruelty springs more terrifyingly than any conventionally 'adult' behaviour. In the Casson/Barker production the delicate balance between the two roles seems to have been upset, for Cathleen Nesbitt's Goneril was felt by more than one critic to be weaker than Fay Compton's Regan – 'icy venom backed by demonic cruelty'.

Perhaps Peter Brook took a hint from a comment by Granville-Barker in his Preface to *Lear*: 'What a good case Goneril makes for herself. . . . And Regan . . . makes an even better case of it.' In any event his 1962 production was notable for the lengths to which it went to justify Goneril and Regan. It is hardly an exaggeration to say that this production endorsed the Goneril/Regan viewpoint, in the manner in which their flattery was made to sound as if they were merely humouring their old father, in the sweetly reasonable tone of their later arguments with Lear and, most notably in showing on stage the unruly behaviour of Lear and his knights, though in the text Lear explicitly denies the charge (see p. 26).

In the action of the play Gloucester is an independent character with his own motivation, prejudices and weaknesses. But in the larger design of the tragedy he is, of course, another Lear figure, enacting in more grossly physical terms the folly and suffering of the tragic hero. The actor and director need to find a balance between these two different aspects. Often this is done by one character 'echoing' at crucial moments the gestures and/or stage position of the other, but sometimes Gloucester acquires a powerful independent reality which may threaten the balance. Sebastian Shaw played Gloucester with such enormous authority in the 1968 Stratford production, as a foolish and well-meaning courtier intent on being friends with everyone if at all possible, that the scene of his blinding came across as the truly appalling shock it ought to be. One professional critic could not bear to watch the scene, while another commented that Shaw's playing threatened to turn the play itself into 'The Tragedy of Gloucester'.

On the other hand, in Peter Brook's 1962 production, Alan Webb's playing of the character as a self-satisfied Polonius-like busybody distanced him from the audience's sympathy. Even in the harrowing torture scene he was left stumbling blindly across the stage, ignored by the servants clearing up around him. In a later scene the blinded Gloucester, crouching on an empty stage and listening to the sounds of battle off-stage,

vividly recalled the dazed Fool crouching and staring unblink-
ingly at Lear battling against the storm. Such visual parallels
may affect the audience in ways not unlike those produced by
the subterranean links among Shakespeare's poetic images.
As noted above, Kozintsev's film literally embodied Lear's
physical strength in the burly physique of the character who
played Gloucester, while at the same time making us more
aware of the affinity between the two characters' fates by
juxtaposition of scenes and the omission of Gloucester's
suicide. The Russian film also stressed the family tension
between Gloucester's two sons by showing a genealogical chart
during Edmund's first soliloquy; and again, when Gloucester's
servants pursue Edgar, by inviting the audience perhaps to
ponder the true significance of family relationships in the play.
The two characters were also played by actors strikingly
similar in appearance. At the very end of the film Edgar leans
against a pillar in a pose similar to that adopted by Edmund for
his first soliloquy, his evident inability to express the depth of
his feelings standing in ironic contrast to the easy fluency of his
half-brother's earlier address.

The 1940 Casson/Barker production rooted Jack Hawkins's
Edmund firmly in Renaissance Machiavellianism: smooth,
glamorous and unashamedly 'theatrical'. This style was also
present in James Booth's portrayal in the Brook production,
but here its effect was disconcertingly out of step as Edmund
appeared to be not smoothly plausible but a larger-than-life
melodramatic villain. Norman Rodway in Nunn's production
did full justice to the exuberant wit of Edmund, an important
quality in the character for it explains not only the sisters'
fascination with him but our own, and reinforces the implied
connection between ease of speech and deviousness of intent.

Edgar's gullibility may be a problem if we see the character
in naturalistic terms and is best considered as a necessary
datum of the play; in any case a plausible Edmund can make it
convincing on the stage. But Edgar's real development occurs
in the tension between his own identity and the role of Poor
Tom which he assumes. The challenge to the actor is to keep
the various 'voices' of Edgar – the frightened brother, the
horrified son, the moralising philosopher, the mad beggar and
the champion of virtue at the end – from lapsing into

incoherence. Not many Edgars have succeeded in modern times in leaving their mark on the play, and both Alan Howard (Stratford 1968) and Brian Murray (Stratford 1962) were criticised as incoherent or colourless, though in fairness it must be said that the Brook production minimised Edgar's importance as it diminished Cordelia's human stature. The view it took of human society did not allow much dignity to it, and it was not only Edgar who suffered but the 'good' characters generally. Kent, who in most productions stands out for his loyalty, courage and plain speaking, emerged here as a sycophantic bully; and Albany, who develops in the play from a timid and even henpecked husband into an outraged fighter for moral decency, caught the audience's attention most strongly when, at the news of Gloucester's blinding, he vomited copiously.

9 SELECTION AND EMPHASIS

Text and Performance

As readers, actors or directors, our knowledge of Shakespeare's dramatic art obviously depends on the text of his plays. But the question, what precisely *is* a Shakespearean text?, is simpler to ask than to answer. There is no evidence that Shakespeare himself was at all interested in the printed versions of his plays, and a good deal to suggest that the acting company of which he was a member was anxious to prevent copies of plays in their possession from reaching the printing house too early in case familiarity affected box-office takings.

In the case of *King Lear* there are two distinct but related texts which are the source of all later editions, one of them generally agreed to be more authoritative than the other. In 1608, two years after the first performance, the play appeared in a quarto (small format) version called the 'Pied Bull' Quarto, after the sign of the printing house from which it originated. Eleven years later came a second Quarto (called the 'Butter' Quarto, after the printer) but this has no independent authority, being clearly derived from a partially corrected copy (see next paragraph) of the 'Pied Bull' Quarto. In 1623, seven years after Shakespeare's death and more than fifteen years after the original staging of the play, *King Lear* was included in the noble First Folio volume gathered together by Shakespeare's fellow-actors, Hemmings and Condell. This, according to their own rather exaggerated editorial claim, 'offered to your view' the texts of the plays 'cured and perfect of their limbs, and all the rest absolute in their numbers as he [Shakespeare] conceived them', not to be confused with the 'divers stolen and surreptitious copies' which had earlier appeared in Quarto format.

This is not the place to enter into details of the relationship between the 1608 and 1623 texts, still less of those between playhouse and printing house in Shakespeare's time. (An excellent summary may be found in the New Penguin edition of the play.) But it needs to be made clear that what the modern reader accepts as Shakespeare's texts is a modern (and occasionally not so modern) editor's version, based on his individual scholarly judgement of the relative authority of the two texts. Each of these is at some distance from Shakespeare's original manuscript. The 1608 Quarto is a generally reliable text, though it is riddled with a number of minor errors caused partly by printers' misreading of the original manuscript, which itself may have been based on actors' memorial recollection of the play augmented by intermittent (and perhaps surreptitious) access to the playhouse prompt copy. The Folio text, generally used as the 'copy text' by most modern editors, was based on a copy of the First Quarto corrected while it was still being printed (as was the time-saving but confusing custom in the Elizabethan printing house), and checked against a playhouse prompt book. It is some 300 lines shorter than the Folio and omits an entire scene [IV iii], but has a hundred lines not found there as well as act and scene divisions, which the Quarto lacks. In general, the Folio text has a simpler line of dramatic action and some of its omissions can be explained on grounds of staging. It is carelessly printed and repeats some of the Quarto's mistakes as well as adding others of its own. It may represent *King Lear* according to stage practice current in the early 1620s when the Folio edition was being prepared.

What all this amounts to is that there is no canonical text which has Shakespeare's own undisputed authority behind it, though textual editors quite properly bring all the considerable resources of modern techniques and even technology to assist their critical judgement in the unceasing search for a text as close as may be to what Shakespeare wrote. The foregoing paragraphs should make it clear that the sources for a modern text themselves ultimately derive from performance rather than the other way about. The 'Pied Bull' Quarto title-page claims that the play is there printed 'as it was played before the King's Majesty at Whitehall upon St Stephen's night in Christmas holidays'. Thus, while the text is all we have, there is nothing sacrosanct about it and the practice of adapting and selecting 'the text' for a particular performance has a precedent dating back to Shakespeare's own theatre. I shall glance briefly at such selection and adaptation as shown in the four productions chosen for discussion.

The 1940 production appears to have followed the guidelines laid down by Granville-Barker himself in the final section of his treatment of the play in *Prefaces to Shakespeare* (1927, with subsequent revisions). It was firmly based on the Folio text and followed it in omitting the scene between Kent and the Gentleman about Cordelia's return to England [IV iii], about which Granville-Barker wrote: 'I could better believe that Shakespeare cut it than wrote it.' As this scene contains a description of Cordelia in quasi-religious terms, its omission would diminish the suggestion of her as a Christ-figure. The production also followed the Folio in cutting some of Edgar's lines as Poor Tom, in assigning the last lines in the play to Edgar rather than Albany, and in omitting the Fool's scene-closing prophecy [III ii], thus maintaining dramatic attention on Lear's spiritual growth. But in three important respects the production departed from the Folio as most subsequent ones have done. First, it restored the mock-trial scene which the Folio omits but which modern critics and directors alike see as a crucial moment in the play. (Trevor Nunn's 1968 production highlighted it with a crazy dance.) Secondly, it restored the dialogue between the two servants at the end of the third act which speaks in the voice of common humanity after the harrowing and inhuman scene of Gloucester's blinding.

Finally, it enhanced the positive stature of Albany by restoring many of his lines which the Folio omits.

Both the Stratford productions took much longer playing time than the Casson/Barker/Gielgud one. Trevor Nunn's took three-and-a-half hours and Peter Brook's nearly four. There were few cuts in either version, but significant ones in the 1962 production were the omission of the moment where the servant tries to save Gloucester from further torture and also the servants' dialogue at the end of the scene. The effect, especially with the interval following immediately after, was to place the emphasis squarely on the idea of the gratuitous and unrelieved inhumanity of man to man. Nunn's production, on the other hand, with its stress on Lear's spiritual fall and redemption and the equal reality of good and evil (roughly paralleled by Danby's notion of the 'two natures' in the play) was widely praised for 'allowing the play to speak for itself' – though it was, inevitably, as much an interpretation as Brook's or any other. Though this production too had a single interval after the blinding scene, the effect here was to arouse the audience to pity rather than to a sort of disinterested horror at the absurdity of existence.

The greater flexibility and freedom of movement allowed by the cinema can be an advantage in putting Shakespeare on film, but the danger of merely trying to find visual equivalents for Shakespeare's language, and thereby rendering it superfluous, is ever-present. Kozintsev, as we have seen, chose not to illustrate Shakespeare's language but to expand its implications in the direction of the social context of the tragedy. The film took its shape, not from act and scene divisions, but according to the cinematic rhythm already described, which follows Lear's progress from isolation to participation in common humanity. The two-part structure divides at the point where Lear goes outdoors [II iv], the second part opening with the storm. The first part emphasises individuals in close-up, while the second is devoted mainly to Lear's own widening vision of man's true place in the world. At several points scenes are rearranged, lines transferred from one context to another and new scenes, such as Cordelia's wedding ceremony, added. Lear's vehement curse against Cordelia – 'Let it be so! Thy truth then be thy dower!' – is not spoken directly indoors but

hurled forth from the castle walls; and his great speech, 'Reason
not the need', is addressed, not to Regan, but outdoors to the
elements, underlining Lear's ordinary humanity and isolation.
The last few moments of the first part show alternating shots of
Lear outdoors in the gathering storm and Edmund holding
Gloucester's astrological charts in his hand – the gathering
storm clouds and the dusty charts binding the two plots
together, both portents of imminent doom.

Leading Ideas

It often seems as if a particular scene or speech in a play has
provided the governing idea behind the whole production,
whether the director has consciously chosen it or not. In the
case of *King Lear* the texture of the play is so rich that there are
innumerable moments which could serve as the keynote of a
production. Almost every scene of the play contains them and
almost every major character utters them. The play cannot be
profitably seen as an anthology of isolated 'great moments'.
Nevertheless, each production highlights certain themes and
underplays others, though the interpretation of the different
themes will ensure that none is wholly lost in an intelligent and
sensitive production.

For Granville-Barker, 'the master-movement of the play,
which enshrines the very soul of the play', begins with Lear's
shedding of the cares of royalty and proceeds unchecked till he
falls into exhausted sleep. The turning-point for Barker comes
when the tormented king finally turns his attention from his
own woes to those of others and kneels down to pray for the
'poor naked wretches'. Kozintsev's film also takes this moment
in the play as its leading motif. 'How, in a word', Kozintsev
asks, 'is one to define the development of the image of Lear?' –
and answers: 'As a thawing. Grief warms him. Disaster melts
the ice; his heart quickens and begins to beat' (*The Space of
Tragedy*, p. 40). But the common perception of the leading idea
begets different emphases in the two interpretations.
Granville-Barker took up Bradley's notion that Lear dies of joy
at the end, believing Cordelia to be alive, and Gielgud
translated this into action so powerfully that the audience's

attention was clearly on Lear's own deluded ecstasy. 'This Lear died on a flare of hope more heart-rending than all the previous agony' (Williamson, p. 136). In the film, on the other hand, the perception of Lear's kinship with the poor of his kingdom dominates the final scene as it does the whole of the second part. We do not see Lear as he cries out 'Howl!' in his final agony, but only hear him as the camera shows us Cordelia's body still hanging; and the final tableau which, on stage invariably focusses attention on Lear and his dead daughter, becomes a shot of the pair glimpsed through a crowd of soldiers. The camera again moves out into the ordinary world: women trying to pick up their daily lives amidst the ruins of war, the Fool playing his desolate tune and almost absent-mindedly kicked by a soldier, Edgar too full of feeling for speech.

The collapse of order in society reflected in the parallel progress in man from clothing to nakedness lay at the heart of Trevor Nunn's 1968 production. Its 'keynote' speech was clearly Lear's 'Off, off, you lendings!', and the chief characters descended to an animal-like harshness of condition as their surroundings decayed from golden pomp to empty darkness. But Lear regained his tragic status at the end, undoubtedly the focus of all eyes on and off stage at his death; and Kent's 'Vex not his ghost', softly uttered, was full of human concern and tenderness. A striking instance of the difference in conception between this production and Peter Brook's of 1962 was seen in the delivery of this very line in the latter. It was shouted peremptorily, as if there was no sense in trying to preserve life in a grotesque and meaningless world, and the only possible happiness lay in the nullity of death. Kozintsev remarks how he realised, when he saw Brook's production in Russia, that these lines had been given 'the greatest significance' as the entire production had striven to project an image of 'the rack of this tough world' on which Kent no longer wished to see his master stretched, a plaything for the wanton gods.

Some Dramatic Highlights

In discussing the problems presented by the play for directors and actors, the imagery of mountain-climbing is often invoked.

Many critics slip into the vocabulary of peaks and precipices, of heights to be scaled and dangerous descents to be negotiated. In an interview with a Stratford newspaper in 1962, Paul Scofield provided his own variation on this terminology. 'To play the last unearthly act', he said, 'Lear must land, as it were, by parachute on top of Parnassus. Mountaineering, however dogged, will not take him there.' The following necessarily brief discussion is devoted to the tackling of some of the 'peaks' in the play in the various productions, though it should never be forgotten that these are not isolated obtrusions but part of a total landscape within which they acquire their meaning and grandeur.

The opening scene is an important 'landmark' for it establishes the dimensions of the protagonist and the nature of the society, sketches the main relationships, and provides the trigger mechanism for the ensuing action. Both Granville-Barker and Trevor Nunn understood the pomp and formality of the occasion: the first in fairly conventional Renaissance terms, the other in a more strikingly 'barbaric' key. Since both saw the main action as Lear's fall from grandeur and the collapse of his society with him, both were obviously concerned to establish that grandeur and the hierarchical value of that society to begin with. In the Nunn production, the magnificent golden tent in which Lear first entered and the white tent of Cordelia echoed each other in shape and function, the only images of human order and stability on the stage. Neither Brook's production nor the Russian film strove for grandeur or formality, though for different reasons. For Kozintsev, Lear's true grandeur came in his suffering, and to begin with he was merely a patriarchal head (we never see him wearing a crown), not to be taken at his own valuation of himself. He was therefore shown before his own fireplace, the attention of all those around him (except Cordelia and the Fool) centred on the map in his hand and the imperious finger tracing the contours of his arbitrary will. Brook's Lear was conceived as an ordinary human being, Everyman rather than Majesty incarnate, and the staging of the opening scene confirmed this view. In contrast to the splendid golden tent in which Eric Porter was borne, Scofield came in through a side-entrance. Before this, the stage had been bare but for a side-table to which Kent, Gloucester and Edmund had gone in turn to fit themselves with gloves and suchlike, accentuating the Brechtian attitude that the audience were to remain detached, observing and judging rather than involved and identified with the action on the stage. The other courtiers came drifting in casually, though once they saw the king they rapidly came to respectful attention. In the 'love game' it was Lear's petulance, and a kind of cunning yet potentially dangerous playfulness, that came through, rather than, as in the film, a sense of the political implications of his wilfulness.

Lear's first confrontation with Goneril and Regan after he has given up his authority is also an important moment, for it marks the beginning of his realisation of the consequences of his folly – and therefore (as Granville-Barker noted), of his dramatic development: 'the master-movement of the play'. The Brook production filled it decisively in favour of the daughters by making Lear and his knights behave in so outrageous a manner that no hostess should have been expected to tolerate it – breaking up the furniture and beating the household servants in their drunken cavortings. The balance of sympathies (such as they were) was so much with the daughters that one reviewer described them as 'a pair of stately Cheltenham sisters suffering the obscene disintegration of their erratic father'. At a corresponding moment Trevor Nunn showed us Lear and his knights engaged in a boar hunt, the trapped boar being baited by the circle of courtiers providing an image which foreshadowed the later condition of Lear himself. The 1940 production appears to have respected the text's neutrality on the subject, stressing Lear's utter astonishment at his reception. Gielgud's rehearsal note against the line, 'Are you our daughter?', reads: 'Blank'; and a few lines after, 'Does any here know me?', is glossed: 'Danger-end of careless exterior. Gasps. Feeling, Speech nothing.' Kozintsev recalls how, at first, he tried to give each actor in Lear's entourage some identifying individuality of character, but abandoned the attempt when he realised that 'these are not people but a representation of a way of life'. In the film Lear's train of knights is extended to a procession which includes a string of carts with trunks, hunting dogs and falcons, but there is no suggestion that the daughters are justified in regarding this as an excessive burden on their households.

For most people the storm scenes contain the very essence of *King Lear*, and productions and performances have been acclaimed or condemned on their rendering of these alone. The scenes are undeniably crucial to the play's meaning and effect, though obviously these are fully apprehended only in the dramatic context. In the older representational convention of the 'picture frame' stage, elaborate realistic scenery dominated the stage, making it necessary for all the storm scenes to be played continuously, with the brief intervening scenes involving Edmund, Gloucester and Cornwall either displaced or omitted. As well as destroying the close interweaving of the two plots, this increased the already enormous physical burden on the actor playing Lear. At the same time, realistic effects of thunder and lightning not only detracted from the actor's efforts to speak his lines audibly, but the whole effort at realism worked against the imaginative identification of the storm outside and within Lear's mind which is the *raison d'être* of the scenes.

Modern productions have been generally more sensitive to the dramatic significance of the storm and less willing to allow these scenes to be used as a designer's and sound effects man's display-window. But Trevor Nunn's production was criticised for an excessive reliance on realistic sound effects, pushing Eric Porter into the trap of ranting in order to outvoice them. One of the problems for the actor is that he must at one and the same time incarnate the storm as well as be its victim. As if this were not demanding enough, Lear also has to topple over convincingly into madness. It is not surprising that male actors regard these scenes as the most challenging in all Shakespeare. Gielgud's rehearsal notes show Granville-Barker's unremitting attention to every word, the careful scoring of the rising movement of Lear's frenzy combined with the avoidance of any attempt at realistic impersonation of the storm. The first notes for the scene are: 'Tune in. Pitch voice. Low key – *Oratorio. Every word impersonal*' (my italics). And the onset of madness is suggested by this: 'Listen tenderly to the Fool, cloak around him (*how nicely you sing*). Hold on to the edge of security. Leave stage on a high, unfinished note' (*Stage Directions*, pp. 25–6). The effect was predictably impressive, and in the words of *The Times* reviewer: 'He [Gielgud] trusts the verse and his power to speak it, as a solitary silver figure in the dark loneliness, *he speaks the storm*, and his trust is never at any vital point betrayed' (my italics).

The film has, of course, its own distinctive techniques for creating the storm, avoiding the temptation of duplicating Shakespeare's words. As a kind of prelude to the storm, we have shots of horses rearing as they are tethered, then wild animals seen through criss-crossing branches, as if caged. Lear himself does not dominate the screen during these scenes but is, at our first glimpse of him, indistinguishable on the horizon. He is seen as one of the 'poor naked wretches' we meet everywhere in the film: anonymous, insignificant beings, ignored by the elements which bear down indifferently on all who are exposed to them, king and beggar alike. The sense of man as victim in an indifferent universe was removed from a historical context and placed in a metaphysical one by Peter Brook. With no sound effects but the occasional rumble of a thunder sheet and on a completely bare brightly-lit stage, Brook 'created' the storm, not only through the highly individual yet immediately striking cadences of Scofield's phrasing, but also through a slow, balletic movement (recalling that of Noh drama) of actors reacting in mime to the buffetings of an imagined storm. Scofield remarked of the director's approach to Lear's madness that 'Brook does not want you to feel Lear's madness but to survey it, understand it, probe it, wrestle with it', which presumably explains the presence of the Fool gazing fixedly at Lear during the storm scenes. It was an interpretation that made staggering demands on actors and audience alike, but they are demands inherent in Shakespeare's own language and dramatic technique.

Before going on to a discussion of the final scene, we may note very briefly how the outlook of each production was reflected in the handling of some other key scenes. The partly indirect depiction of the blinding of Gloucester in the film, the clinical detachment of Brook's version, and the enormous sympathy for suffering generated by Sebastian Shaw in Nunn's 1968 Stratford production were all highly characteristic of the respective interpretations. The 'Dover cliff' scene, omitted from the film (presumably because it was rightly felt to be ineradicably rooted in the theatre), was understandably one of the high points of the Brook production, for it provided a theatrical metaphor for the conception which guided the entire production. This conception has been formulated by Jan Kott. After remarking that the scene could only succeed on a flat, bare stage, he continues: 'Gloucester's suicide has meaning only if the gods exist. . . . Its sole value lies in its reference to the absolute. . . . But if the gods and their moral order do not exist, Gloucester's suicide. . . . is only a somersault on an empty stage' (see Kott's essay in the Casebook on the play, p. 277). Finally, the scene of Lear's awakening to music in Cordelia's care was one of the great moments in the 'heroic' and 'humanist' versions of the play offered by Granville-Barker and Trevor Nunn respectively. In the film it is not an intimate moment but almost a public one, with the screen image including the Fool and soldiers in the background. In Peter Brook's version the scene went for almost nothing. The symbolic value of new garments was not realised on stage and the absence of music was never so keenly felt, while, as befits an interpretation which saw no real possibility of human regeneration, Lear himself seemed never to have recovered sanity or serenity.

The attitudes implied here carried over to the handling of the great final scene in each version. The 'flare of hope' in which Lear died in the 1940 production was carefully prepared for by the dreadful ferocity of the earlier 'Howl, howl!', the almost carefree jollity of 'I have seen the day', the sudden sadness of 'I am old now', and the abrupt cry of genuine discovery on 'Pray you, undo this button'. These comments are all derived from Gielgud's rehearsal notes, which end with the single word: 'Joy.' The note of joy was more muted in Trevor Nunn's production, while the film pulls away from the tableau of the personal tragedy to show the bodies of Lear and Cordelia, together with those of Goneril and Regan, carried across the stage, and then moves further out into shots of ordinary living, leaving us at the end with the literally speechless Edgar. The most strikingly original emphasis came, as we might expect, in Peter Brook's production. Scofield's playing of the last scene was undoubtedly moving, but any vestige of possible joy or hope was rigorously excluded by Kent's vehement cry of 'Vex not his ghost!' as we heard once more the faint rumble of thunder: a reminder that this conclusion, given the view taken of human fate, had concluded nothing.

10   CONCLUSION

The reader will have noticed some overlapping both between Parts One and Two and within the separate sections of each part. This is unavoidable, but I have also made no special effort to avoid it, though I hope mere repetition is minimal. *King Lear* is above all things a unified whole, although admittedly one of a distinctive if not unique kind; the categories of analytical criticism will repeatedly come into collision with this unity. At the same time discussion of theatrical interpretation will reflect critical preoccupations. It is part of the express purpose of this book, as of the others in the series, that the reflection should be coherent and deliberate.

In Part One an attempt is made not only to identify the central concerns of *King Lear* but to show how these are realised in the developing pattern of the play and related to the pattern of other Shakespearean tragedies. The dominant oppositions of the play – folly and wisdom, blindness and insight, language and silence, quality and quantity – are traced through the interplay of imagery, character and action. Part Two tries to show how four different conceptions of the play – which may briefly and crudely be termed Heroic, Humanist, Historical and Absurdist – result in differences of emphasis and arrange ment. While specific details are offered to illustrate general points as far as space permits, no attempt has been made to describe each production in all its aspects. I have also tried to avoid obtruding my own judgement of each production, though I have expressed my admiration for the film at the outset. Each production has been seen as a series of practical choices as regards costume and setting, the physical appearance of characters, their relative positions on stage and related matters. If the reader returns to *King Lear* with a sense of its richness and variety, of its language and action as part of a unified whole which can only be fully realised in theatrical terms, while at the same time being aware of how much scope for responsible imaginative interpretation the play offers, this brief study will have served its purpose.

READING LIST

A. C. Bradley's essay on *King Lear* in *Shakespearean Tragedy* – originally published in 1904 and repeatedly reprinted (Macmillan, London; St Martin's Press, New York) – is invaluable for the richness of the author's imaginative response and for crucially influential interpretations of certain moments in the play. Bradley's occasional over-emphasis on character distinct from the world it inhabits is a small price to pay for the continuously illuminating critical perception he shows.

Equally important, chiefly for the theatrical perspective which Bradley virtually ignores (believing the play to be unactable), is Harley Granville-Barker's *Preface* to the play, first published in 1930, revised in 1935 and in print ever since. It is part of the 6-volume *Prefaces to Shakespeare* (1927–47), now available in paperback (Batsford, London, 1969–74).

Jan Kott's *Shakespeare Our Contemporary* (Methuen, London, 1964; Norton, New York, 1964) had an immense vogue when it first appeared, especially among theatre people. It is still stimulating even if, or perhaps because, it persistently overstates its case. The essay, '*King Lear*, or Endgame', is one of the best in the book. It should be read together with G. Wilson Knight's chapter on the play in *The Wheel of Fire* (Methuen, London, 1930), from which it partly derives.

Grigori Kozintsev's *King Lear: The Space of Tragedy* (London, Heinemann, 1972) is a fascinating combination of literary and theatrical criticism, film diary, autobiography and philosophical reflection. No reader can fail to understand *King Lear* more deeply after reading it. It is illustrated with stills from Kozintsev's film of 1970.

R. B. Heilman's *This Great Stage* (Louisiana State UP, Baton Rouge, 1948) is a book-length study of the play, concentrating on patterns of imagery.

Maynard Mack's *King Lear in Our Time* (University of California Press, 1965; paperback 1972) contains some deeply considered criticism of the play, as well as trenchant questioning of some modern attempts to provide it with 'relevance' in the theatre.

Excerpts from Bradley, Mack, Kott and Heilman, along with several other studies, are included in *King Lear: A Casebook*, edited by Frank Kermode; this has a fuller bibliography than can be given here.

INDEX OF NAMES

FOR READER'S NOTES

FOR READER'S NOTES

FOR READER'S NOTES

TEXT AND PERFORMANCE

General Editor: Michael Scott

The series is designed to introduce students to the themes, continuing vitality and performance of major dramatic works. The attention given to production aspects is an element of special importance, responding to the invigoration given to literary study by the work of leading contemporary critics.

The prime aim is to present each play as a vital experience in the mind of the reader – achieved by analysis of the text in relation to its themes and theatricality. Emphasis is accordingly placed on the relevance of the work to the modern reader and the world of today. At the same time, traditional views are presented and appraised, forming the basis from which a creative response to the text can develop.

In each volume, Part One: *Text* discusses key themes or problems, the reader being encouraged to gain a stronger perception both of the inherent character of the work and also of variations in interpreting it. Part Two: *Performance* examines the ways in which these themes or problems have been handled in modern productions, and the approaches and techniques employed to enhance the play's accessibility to modern audiences.

A synopsis of the play is given, and an outline of its major sources, and a concluding Reading List offers guidance to the student's independent study of the work.

PUBLISHED